From a Hustler's Woman
to the
Pastor's Wife
The Story of First Lady
Carrie A. Williams

Life To Legacy, LLC

From A Hustler's Woman, to the Pastor's Wife
By: Carrie A. Williams

ISBN-10: 1939654173
ISBN-13: 978-1-939654-17-5

Printed in the United States
10 9 8 7 6 5 4 3 2 1

Cover concept by: Carrie A. Williams

Cover design by: Lewis Lee

Literary consultation services provided by:
Dr. Dennis J. Woods

Published by:
Life To Legacy, LLC
2441 Vermont Street, #57
Blue Island, IL 60406
(877) 267-7477
www.Life2Legacy.com

To Glen
Thank you for
your support I
love you enjoy.
Carrie A Williams
8-5-2014

To contact the author send email to:
Carriesunique@yahoo.com

To purchase this book go to
Amazon.com or BN.com

CONTENTS

DEDICATION

This book is dedicated to my wonderful mother Flora N. Johnson, who made her transition on December 19, 2011. In her tireless loving way she insisted that we be the best that we could be in all that we did. She was a light for our entire family, and set a firm example for us all to follow.

To my stepfather Jonnie L. Johnson, who is a champion in my life.

To my handsome husband District Elder Anthony Williams, Sr., Pastor of Labor of Love Apostolic Church, of Chicago Illinois, you are my man who stands so tall in my life. You once preached a sermon titled, "Finish What You Started," which inspired me and still inspires me in everything that I do. I thank you from the bottom of my heart for being the love of my life. I never knew what love was until I found Jesus and you. Love you always.

ACKNOWLEDGMENTS

I would like to acknowledge the following individuals for their love, encouragement, and support throughout my life's journey. You make each day of my life brighter and give me a reason to always be the best person that I can be. To my children; Michael Romeo, Natemeia (Candice), Annie, Katrina, Tony Jr., Tarsha, all my aunties and uncles. To my grandchildren; Jade, Justys, Jeremy, A'mya, King, Rain, and Tiera. To Coliss, Cheryl, Carol, Fola Shade, Jackie, Carolyn & Robert James (2014), and Darlene. To all of Carrie's Unique clients. To our Labor of Love Apostolic Church family. To my sisters Diane, Shelly, Michelle, Margretta, and brothers Willie (Karen) and Dennie. To all my nieces, nephews, and cousins, you are too many to acknowledge here individually, but you know I love you all. To Lady K, who was inspiring me to "hurry up and finish." My favorite cousin Shelia, and Shawn. To my spiritual mom Dr. Carolyn Starling and Irene Bibbie who modeled me as a new babe in Christ. To Donna Smith-Salmon my girl. To my Auntie Elizabeth who always helped me to keep the faith and was always there to help pull us through. Vickie who sat in my seat and begin to type and help line things up. And to Tabitha, Rashonda and Teresa, and to everyone I was unable to name here—I love you all.

Finally, to all of the hard working and dedicated first ladies who serve the Lord, their husbands, and their congregations. May God bless and keep you in Jesus' mighty name.

PREFACE

I am writing this book on behalf of women everywhere. No matter where you live or what neighborhood you grew up in, it doesn't matter—I'm writing this book for you. This book is for every woman who sought fulfillment in toxic relationships, waiting for the validation that never seems to come. And for every grown woman who harbors a broken hearted little girl on the inside, who never recovered from the hurt of the past.

I'm writing this book for the women who have yet to experience that dreams don't always come true and that nightmares can quickly become a way of life. For every woman who thought that if they just had the right man, or pursued the right career that they would be on the road to happiness. I'm telling my story for every woman who thought that money and material things determine who they are, only to find out that materialism leads to spiritual bankruptcy.

I am writing this book for every woman who lays their head on tear stained pillows because a troubled heart won't let them rest. This book is also for all the women who are haunted by the guilt of the past, confronting the lingering memories of yesterday's sins. So many women are tempted to compromise for sensual desire that has a few moments of pleasure but leads to a lifetime of consequences and pain. My book is for every woman on the cusp of making that devastating life altering decision, to warn her to be careful of the paths you choose in life. I'm reaching out to every woman who bought into the myth that experience is the best teacher only to find that things experienced can never be undone.

I'm writing this book for all the lonely women out there, to inform you that you are not alone, because the Lord said; "He will never leave or forsake you." There is no trauma so deep or transgression so terrible, that the Lord cannot heal and make you whole again. No matter how twisted you have become, the Lord will unravel you and wrap you in His loving arms. Jesus will lovingly lead you to the place that He called you to be, because He's the one with the master plan for your life.

The Lord declares, "For I know the plans I have for you," declares the LORD, "plans to prosper you and not to harm you, plans to give you hope and a future" (Jer. 29:11 NIV). But beware, the devil also has a plan for your life, and it will not work out for your good. He is the thief who comes only to steal, kill, and to destroy.

The enemy attempted to steal my identity in exchange for a counterfeit life so I would never become whom God intended for me to be. That's why I'm writing this book, to warn you about the devil's scheme to have you assume the wrong identity. But fear not, and be of good courage because greater is He that is in us than he that is in the world. Faithful is our God. He is the author and finisher of our faith and your latter days shall be greater than your past.

INTRODUCTION

One of my favorite Gospel stories is the account found in Luke chapter 7, about a woman who came to worship the Lord as he dined at a Pharisee's house. This powerful account illustrates several very important spiritual concepts that are essential in a dynamic relationship with God. The Bible informs us that as Jesus sat down to eat, a sinful woman, entered the Pharisee's home and began worshiping the Lord. The text tells us that she washed Jesus' feet with her tears, wiped his feet with her hair, kissed his feet, and then anointed his feet with expensive oil from her alabaster box.

This account is one of the most profound examples of a person exhibiting a broken spirit and a contrite heart in the entire Bible. Who this woman was is not important, but what is important is that we know she was a sinner who through humility and a broken heart found deliverance there at the Lord's feet. Obviously, this woman was not interested in form and fashion. She did not concern herself with religious protocol or etiquette. No, she put all that aside, because being in the immediate presence of the Lord was more important to her.

As I pondered over this text, I was amazed at the reaction of the Pharisee who reasoned within himself, "If Jesus were a prophet, he would have known that this woman touching him is a sinner." Yes, that old Pharisee, "a self-righteous one," criticized a poor soul who had come to Jesus for deliverance. If it were left up to him, he would have never let her in to see Jesus. He would have turned her away at the door just because she was a sinner.

Jesus, knowing what was in his heart responded to the Pharisee's contempt for the woman saying, "I have something to say to you." Then Jesus told the parable of the two debtors, who owed a collector some money. One of the debtors owed a little, and the other one owed a lot. The collector outright forgave both men their debts. Jesus asked the Pharisee, which one will love the collector the most? The Pharisee responded, "The one who owed the most." Jesus responded, "You're right." Then he went on to say, "Her sins, which are many, are forgiven; for she loved much: but to whom little is forgiven, the same loveth little." Wow, what a powerful and tremendous spiritual truth. I can identify with this woman. That woman might as well have been me—a woman simply known as a sinner, who poured out her heart as she worshiped at the feet of Jesus.

So when I got saved, I wanted my heart to be clean, and I wanted God to renew in me a right spirit. I wanted to be saved for real, all the way, the right way. I did not want any of that superficial, outward appearance stuff like the Pharisee. I wanted a real relationship with the Master. I said to the Lord, please don't let me become one of those stone faced, frowned up, dress down to the ankles, self-righteous types, who scare people away from the church. No, I wanted to exhibit the love of God to everyone. But most importantly, just as the woman in Luke who washed Jesus' feet with her tears, and wiped His feet with her hair, I wanted to serve God in Spirit and truth.

Jesus said, the Pharisees or self-righteous folks, are like "whited sepulchers that indeed appear beautiful outward, but are within full of dead men's bones...." No, I wasn't just looking for an outward religious experience. I wanted a dynamic relationship with the Lord, because He had forgiven me so much. Therefore, with all my heart, I love Him much. He gave me another chance and much better life than the one I led for too long.

As we all know, life is like taking a long journey. There's so many winding roads, pitfalls and potholes, twists and turns, unexpected detours, and perilous conditions. Yes, through it all, we make it to our destiny. As with all of us, we want to know "Who am I" and what is my purpose in life? Where we look for those answers, will determine the road that we travel. As you will discover while reading my story, the path that we walk, is often not a path that we always choose. But God, in His awesome providence guides us to the place He has called us to be. He is the author and finisher of our faith.

In Psalm 37:23-24, David writes: "The steps of a good man are ordered by the LORD: and he delighteth in his way. Though he fall, he shall not be utterly cast down: for the LORD upholdeth him with his hand." I have found, no matter whether we understand this or not, it is true. Our steps are ordered by God. We have all questioned our paths in life. When unfortunate things occur, and we ask "why," we are really trying to make sense out of something bad or unexplainable. As hard as we try to understand the "whys" of life, we must learn to take comfort in the fact that God knows, even if we never know.

We all go through difficulties in life. But we all have different stories and each one of us must walk their own path. Everyone has a story, but as the refrain from the hymn, Blessed Assurance says, "...this is my story, this is my song...." Truly that's what this book is my story. I am writing it so that someone else can be encouraged and strengthened. I am writing this book to encourage people to not give up, and to keeping trust in God. Remember, your steps have already been ordered.

God has brought me a mighty long way. Today, I am a survivor, an overcomer, delivered and set free by the hands of Almighty God. I am the First Lady of the Labor of Love, Apostolic Church of Chicago, Illinois. I am happily married to District Elder Anthony Williams, Sr. Today; I am a role-model and a living testimony for women out there who are still struggling to find their way in life. I'm here to tell you to be strong and stand tall, because no matter what you have been through, God has a master plan for your life.

Chapter 1

In The Beginning

"Therefore judge nothing before the time, until the Lord come
… and then shall every man have praise of God."
1 Corinthians 4:5

I was born, April 12, 1964, in a small town called Brockton, Massachusetts. Brockton is about 25 miles south of Boston. Like many small towns, most people probably have never heard of Brockton. It's not known for much. If you look up Brockton online, you will discover that it has the distinction of being one of the windiest cities in America. Ironically, after the first six years of my life, my family moved to a big concrete jungle, Chicago, also known as "The Windy City."

I grew up in a fairly large family. Altogether, there were eight of us; my mom and dad, and six children. I am the fourth child out of a sibship of four girls and two boys. My father was a man with a lot of problems. He was not a good role model. From my recollection, he always stayed in trouble with the law and even did time in jail for almost stabbing a man to death. To be around my father put us all in peril.

Due to the bad vibes that seemed to cling to my father, my mother did everything she could to shield our family from trouble. Therefore, every summer my mother would send my siblings and me down south to another small town called Pachuta, Mississippi. And it wasn't long after those sweltering hot summers, amongst the red dirt and tall pines of rural Mississippi, that my mother finally became fed-up with my father. So, once and for all, she left him.

By the time I was six years old, momma moved us to Chicago. The move did us all some good. Finally, we were away from all the insanity and instability created by my wayward father. With him out of our lives, all the chaos was gone. My mother didn't stay single long. She married a man that finally showed me what a father looked like. And ever since then, he has been the only father figure that I have ever known. He would serve as my first positive male role model. Unfortunately, even at a tender young age, I had already been infected with bad men syndrome. I would encounter a series of other bad men in my life that were of lesser caliber than my step-dad.

After getting settled and nestled into our humble little home, we all started going to church. The church we attended was a large high-spirited church on Chicago's Southside, named Cross Temple Church of God in Christ. Being a young child at the time, I guess you could say I enjoyed going to church even though I didn't understand a lot of what went on there. Cross Temple was a very lively Pentecostal church; seems like the same people would get "happy," every

14

Sunday. For the life of me I could not figure out why they were jumping all over the place, causing the ushers to hold them down. Yet, others would run around the church. It all seemed so bizarre. Among my favorite recollections of the church was the choir, and how they sang so beautifully. They would sing hymns that really stirred your soul. And of course, the pastor would preach powerful sermons. But the one thing that stood out most was, people speaking in tongues. This was a little frightening to me because I didn't understand a word that they were saying. And, I would soon find out that no one else did either.

Nevertheless, rain, sleet, or snow, whenever the doors of the church were open, we were there no matter what. My mother used to line us all up, and together we'd all walk to the bus stop and wait on the bus to take us to church. We weren't like most families that only went to church on Sunday morning. No-sir-re, we were at church every Wednesday and Friday night too. This was how it was in our household, week end and week out—year in and year out.

However, by the time I reached my teen years, around the age of fourteen, there was a sudden shift in my parent's spirituality. Both my mother and stepfather backslid and stopped attending church. And to be honest with you, that was just fine with us kids. So, when my parents' backslid, so did us kids. Church stopped having a prominent place in our lives. Although we may have been through with God, God wasn't through with us—not by a long shot.

Despite our sudden lapses in faith, we still grew up in a very nice stable home. My parents were very dedicated to doing the best they could to provide for us, and raise us properly. We weren't rich by any means. We were really a poor family, but my mother never let us know how poor we really were. She never allowed us to even think that we were poor. However, when I look back, I realize that we were in poverty. Momma could only shop at thrift stores, and discount department stores like, Community's, and Zayers—in comparison to some of our cousins, who were shopping in more expensive stores like Carson Pirie Scott.

No matter where she shopped, my mother made sure that we always looked our best. She took very good care of us. I remember in second grade my mother bought me these cute little walking suits that everyone would complement me on. So even back in elementary school, I was looking like a well-to-do little princess, but in reality, momma struggled to buy the very clothes on my back.

I can remember times when momma didn't have a quarter to split between us. But being the proud dignified woman that she was, she refused to let us know that she didn't have money for school. So, whenever she was broke, and we came in to ask her for school money, momma would pretend to be sleep. She wouldn't move a muscle or utter a sound, no matter how hard we shook her. It was her way of avoiding telling us that she didn't have any money to give us. I'm sure she felt bad as it was already. She just couldn't bring herself to saying it. So, a few minutes of shaking her and no response, her silence spoke louder than words, and we would give up and walk out of the room. It was sad occasions like these that bred determination in me. And as I took that twenty-block walk to school, I would say to myself, if it is the last thing that I do, I will make sure that my mother never wants for anything.

While growing up, one thing never changed, I was always the smallest. That meant that I received my sisters' hand-me-down clothes. I'm sure at one point or another I wore each one of my sisters' clothes. Boy, did I hate looking like them. An outfit that my mother bought for one of my older sisters, that looked good on them, meant I'd be wearing it a few years down the line. And, it didn't matter if someone else knew it or not—I did. So, I said, "When I get older, I am not going to dress like anybody in my family or anybody else." To this day, I can say I really don't dress like anyone else. I set my own style. I spoke it back then, and by the grace of God, I have the means to walk in that reality. Each day, I thank God for my uniqueness and my individuality. In times like these where everyone is trying to be like someone else, I celebrate and fully embrace who God has created me to be.

My mother and stepfather wanted us to be individuals of integrity. They only wanted the best for us. They made sure we went to school. They did their best to make sure we stayed out of trouble. That's why family time was so important. We ate dinner together as a family, just about six o'clock every evening. While eating we'd talk about our activities of the day or an occasional current event. Dinner time was not only family bonding time, but also a time of wholesome teachable moments. After dinner, when we went outside to play, there was none of that coming in at all times of night. We had to be in the house when the streetlights came on. However, with all of my parent's efforts to create a wholesome family environment, by the time I was a teenager, I took a detour from being "little girl," and I started down the road to rebellion. As a result, I turned out to be the wildest child of all my siblings. My mother had to stay on me. She couldn't let up on me at all. And I know that there were many nights that she had to pray for me, because I was clearly headed in the wrong direction. It wasn't long before I was labeled the "black sheep" of the family.

As one could expect, my siblings often played on my waywardness, because as long as I was the one getting into trouble, it kept the spotlight off of them. "Momma, guess what she done did now." I was always in the spotlight. Problem was, I didn't mind being in the spotlight. My other issue was, my mouth. Give me half a chance and I'd smart off in a second. I just had to have the last word on everything. My mom had a quick remedy for my "last word syndrome"—a slap right across the mouth. Maybe I was overcompensating with lip, for what I lacked in size. But whatever the reason, being outspoken was the way I was assured that I would be heard and not ignored.

Standing up for myself often meant I had to get physical with my brothers and sisters. I was quite a rabble-rouser. I think I fought all my brothers and sisters except one, my eldest sister, I was scared of her. Since she was so much older than me she was more of a mother figure than a sister. But anybody else, I would fight in a minute. Looking back at it, it was how I coped with being the smallest child. So, I learned, at an early age the way to keep people off of you, was to be ready to fight. It's the scared ones who always got picked on. That wasn't going to be me.

Being the typical rambunctious kids, there were times we fought like cats and dogs. However, don't be an outsider who dared put their hands on either one of us. I remember while growing up my mother taught us that if we had to fight some-body, it was not to be one-on-one, it was to be six against one. If you mess with me, you messed with all my brothers and sisters. It was one for all and all for one. That's how momma taught us. She would dare us to come back home crying and whining about we got whipped by some bully. Momma didn't like us starting any fights. She'd much rather us to come home telling her we finished a fight that someone else started.

Now, by no means am I advocating violence, because there is too much fighting and bullying going on in schools and in our communities today. But I'm telling you how my mother raised us, during a time that has since long passed away.

Growing up on the Southside of Chicago was fertile ground for trouble. On the days that I didn't cut class, I attended Calumet High School, located in the Auburn Gresham neighborhood of Chicago. School was cool, because that's where I could meet up with my friends. But even amongst friends, there is a pecking order—I had the need to be out front. I always felt that I had to prove myself to others—that I could do things with or without them. I was so obstinate. If someone told me no, I said "yes." If someone told me yes, I said "no." If someone told me that I couldn't do something, I'd go out of my way just to prove them wrong. That defiant attitude led me straight to the school of hard knocks. I was trying to live life in the fast lane, I even ended up in jail a couple of times and my mother had to come and bail me out. I just couldn't get enough of hanging out with the wrong crowd. I was the typical teenager who swore by their friends.

Pretty soon, I started turning my attention to boys. But I didn't want no little choir boy—a goody two shoes, scared of getting his hands dirty. If he wasn't naughty, I didn't want him. He had to have fine clothes, a nice car and money in his pockets.

I'm not sure where all of this came from. Maybe it was because when I was twelve years old, I was sexually molested by a trusted family member. As the typical molester does, he took time to groom me. While my mother and father were away, he would be there with my sister and me all alone, but his attention was focused on me. That's what he liked, to be alone with us. He used to call me up to the front of the house. There he would be sitting on the living room couch. With a sinister look in his eyes and reeking of cheap whiskey, under the influence of the liquor and the devil, he lusted after my innocent young body.

20

He would always start by telling me to come sit on his lap. This was uncomfortable because I could feel him. Then soon he would start fondling me all over. Then he would start rubbing my private parts. I knew what he was doing was wrong. But, like so many young girls in my predicament, I said nothing. I kept it a secret. Mainly because I knew if my mother found out, she would have gone to jail for killing him. Not wanting my mother to be taken away from us, my own fear and guilt worked against me and provided all the cover that the perpetrator needed to keep doing his evil.

Not only does being molested cause shame and guilt, but another side effect is that you start acting out. Molestation haunts you because you can't erase those terrible memories. You can't undo the experience where you are stimulated by an illegitimate action that so deeply violates you. Oddly, there is a part of you that despises the action, but there's another part of you that becomes aroused. Unfortunately, these types experiences can cause you to follow the wrong paths in life.

As for that relative molester, when I was fifteen years old, I found out that he had died. That was one of the happiest days of my life, because it meant that a bad character in a difficult chapter of my life, was gone forever. I have long moved past those days, only looking back now to tell my story, but he will never have control over me again, because as the Bible says, "Who the Son sets free, is free indeed." Though the perpetrator never knew it, I thank God, that I forgive him before he died. I didn't want to drag him along any further in my life having unresolved anger dogging my footsteps.

Nevertheless, experiences like that affected me as I was growing up. I became more daring—pushing the limits, living on the edge. Though I loved experiencing the excitement of the fast life, I was really setting myself up to be deceived. It all stemmed from wanting so badly to be noticed and loved. That's why I was so head strong. That's why I thought I knew everything. That's why I wouldn't listen to wise counsel. That's why I had to be seen and heard, and always have the last word. I was stuck on myself. Me, myself and I, is what I was all about. But I was too blind, too inexperienced to play in the devil's playground. I was going too fast in the wrong direction. I was searching intently for something that wasn't really there. I was trying so hard to feed that strong inner passionate desire to be fulfilled. To be a woman, that's what I wanted. And where I was standing, the road I was on, being a woman meant I had to have a man. But that's what led me to fall into the arms of four different men—each one a different chapter in my life and a different chapter in this book.

I ended up in a relationship with a man that I thought had it all together and truly cared for me. But, I was wrong. Yes he had plenty of game and plenty of money. I was taken in by the fancy car and sharp clothes. Yeah, it happens all the time to young girls who think they are old enough to play with the big boys. But on these unforgiving streets, you can end up with a broken heart, pregnant, on drugs or even worse—dead.

Chapter 2

ALL THAT GLITTERS…
THE FIRST HUSTLER: MR. ICE

For wisdom is better than rubies; and all the things that may be desired are not to be compared to it. How much better is it to get wisdom than gold! and to get understanding rather to be chosen than silver!
Proverbs 8:11,16:16

Today, we live in a world that is consumed with materialism and the pursuit of wealth and riches. To obtain these things, many have compromised their morals, self dignity, and have even sold their souls to the devil. The messages that we receive through various media outlets, commercials and particularly secular music and movies, reinforces this idea that riches and success should be the chief pursuit of life. However, nothing could be further from the truth—it's all a satanic lie. In Romans 12:2 the Bible tells us not to be conformed to this world, but to be transformed by the renewing of your mind. Conformity to the secular world's ways will lead you down the broad road to deception and destruction.

When you are young and gullible you are not aware of all of the pitfalls of life. Being precocious and inexperienced is a dangerous combination. When you're young, and think you know everything, the last thing that the average teenager wants is their parent's wisdom. However, having that wisdom will help you avoid a whole lot of trouble in life. It is often said that experience is the best teacher. Well, I beg to differ. Whereas, experience is a practical teacher, it certainly is not the best teacher. The best teacher comes from hearing wisdom from someone else who has already walked your path. The best wisdom is to learn from someone else's mistakes, so you don't have to make the same errors. As I would find out at the age of sixteen, some mistakes change your life forever.

At the tender age of sixteen I was trying to live life in the fast lane, where the allure of superficial things was irresistible. I didn't understand that all that glitters was not gold. It hadn't sunk in yet that you can't always believe what you see. But when I was young, I was easily impressed by material things. Show me a fancy car, some sharp clothes and the bling-bling, I would really think you were in to something. So that's how I got started with my first man, whom I will call Mr. Ice, my first hustler.

As far as I could tell, Mr. Ice had it going on. He had a nice car, dressed well, and most importantly he had money in his pockets. The odd thing was, he didn't have a job. He wasn't punching anyone's clock. That alone should have been a big red flag, but, like I said, I thought I knew everything.

Though he had a beeper on his side, he wasn't a doctor, but he did have a clientele where all the customers seem to have the same name—John. Mr. Ice was a pimp. At the time, I didn't think much about it, besides, who was I to judge? Anyway, he always took care of me. There were even times when my mother needed a little help, she wouldn't ask me for anything, but I made sure whoever my man was at the time, gave extra so I could help my mother.

Ironically, Mr. Ice didn't come from a pimp's pedigree, but from a stable and cultured background. His father was a business owner who had been employed by the CTA (Chicago Transit Authority) from where he retired after thirty years of service. Ice was the only boy—so he was spoiled. There wasn't anything that he couldn't get from his parents. He attended the best Catholic grammar and high schools, so he received a good education. But as Ice got older, the straight and narrow life was putting him to sleep. He was itching for excitement and was enticed by the street life. As far as Mr. Ice was concerned, punching a clock was for chumps and suckers.

I met Mr. Ice during my freshman year at Calumet High School, as he was walking through the hallways. I guess he attracted my attention because it was obvious to me that he didn't belong there. Stature wise, he was the smallest one of the group, but status wise; he was the leader of a small group of four or five guys. When I saw him I made the same mistake that Eve made in the garden. Mr. Ice was the forbidden fruit, which I just had to have. In my lusting naive heart I said, "He is fine and I can see him being mine." I was determined to be with him. And even though it took some doing, after a while we began dating.

Like most relationships that are doomed to fail, things started off well. But, Mr. Ice was not satisfied with the mundane life that his parents and structured upbringing dictated. No, that wasn't enough for him. He wanted more, but he didn't want to get it the right way. He began to sell cocaine, marijuana, and hash. Not wanting to deal with the obvious perils of the illicit drug trade, he switched gears into a lower-risk occupation, so he opened up his own newspaper stand, selling various scented incenses and different rolling papers. That venture did well for a while, but that wasn't enough action for him either, so he gave up on that too.

Hopping out of the frying pan into the skillet, Mr. Ice next directed his enterprising efforts into sex-trafficking. Or, like we said it back in those days, he started pimping. He certainly was very enterprising and he built up a big clientele by having a diverse group of women. His first group of female commodities consisted of a Caucasian girl who he called, "Snow White," an Asian descent girl, who went by the name, "China Doll," and a big-hipped sister-girl. I had to be in the house by ten o'clock, which is the time he had to be out supervising his workers, so I wasn't in the car with him while he was hustling. However, he never tried to hide it from me. He was real honest and open with me.

When Mr. Ice first came to my neighborhood, he let everybody know that I belonged to him. The brothers knew I was off limits. They were paranoid because of Mr. Ice. They would say, "Girl, that crazy man you got, he's probably some-where hiding in the bushes checking us out now." None of the guys would take any chances; he made sure I was off limits.

On one occasion I had just bought some food at Church's Chicken and this young man started messing with me. He snatched my chicken out of my hand. I wasn't in the mood to argue with him, so I went and got Ice. Ice confronted the brother and beat him so badly that I was scared for the poor guy and myself. Ice was that brutal of a man. I should have left him then, but I didn't. His actions both terrified and thrilled me at the same time—so I pursued our relationship. But after that, nobody would ever mess with me knowing that this man was in my life. That's how afraid and fearful they were of him.

With all of his explosive rage and propensity for violence, he wasn't a woman beater. He would just try to talk or hold you down. I was the wild one. I fell in love with him, not knowing what real love was, or knowing who I was falling in love with. Like any relationship, we had some good times and we also had some tough times. The rough times were when he wanted to follow his wandering eye, or when I still wanted to be momma's little girl.

It's interesting, why exactly do we choose who we do to be our mate? As I later came to understand, a girl's first image of a man, whether good or bad, comes from the relationship or lack thereof, which she has with her father. In my case, my father was a thug. And his image had been imprinted deep within me. Whether I tried to escape it or embrace it, like a broken compass his image led me to pursue the wrong, Mr. Right. That's why I sought who I did, and that's why I was lashing out so much. I was angry, and in search of the right man to heal the pain of a bruised heart.

Mr. Ice turned out to be quite ambitious. He took his three women all the way to Iowa. Apparently the trip was well worth it, because he came back with a whole lot of money. With some of that money he bought me some expensive jewelry and some very nice coats. These gifts had a way of easing the reservation I had about his business. Prostitutes I could deal with because it was strictly business between him and them. But the fact that he was two-timing me with another chick on the side, didn't sit well with me at all. At first I didn't make the connection on what to expect from a man like Mr. Ice. After all, if he was a pimp, fidelity obviously wasn't one of his strong character traits.

I didn't know much, but I knew I didn't want to continue living like this. Soon things became very rocky with us. I always did have a mouth on me. I had no shortage of words voicing my dislikes, so we began arguing all the time. One time while driving down the street our arguing became so contentious; of all places we stopped the car on some railroad tracks and were going at it. Evidentially, someone called the police. Once the cops arrived, instead of chilling out, he got mad with the police and tried fighting them. Well they weren't having it, so they arrested him on the spot; handcuffs and all. He went completely off and wouldn't shut his mouth. He even threatened to whip each officer one at a time. I'm surprised they didn't try to arrest me as well, considering I had scratched him up so bad. But as soon as those handcuffs were on him, I ran home to my mother.

It wasn't long before he bailed himself out and came to my house looking for me. My mother and father were sitting on the porch, I was in the house. My parents suspected that he may try coming to the house, so they were sitting outside on the porch. Lo and behold, there he came pulling up. My parents knew he was a wild something. After walking up on the porch, it was obvious that he had been in a fight. He asked my mother to tell me to come to the door. She told him, "I don't think you want her to come to this door. You already look like someone who has been in a cat fight, so I'm sure that you don't want to come through this door." While they were talking I was on the inside behind the door laughing. After seeing he wasn't getting anywhere, he got in his car and drove away.

He called me later, just as I suspected that he would. He tried to explain the reason for everything that had transpired. He was very remorseful and rightfully so, because this time, it really wasn't my fault.

Despite that big blowout, I still had deep feelings for him. Clearly, I was not one of his girls that he could control. Maybe that's what he really liked about me. I was spunky and stood up to him. I made him earn my love and devotion. But he was older, street wise and knew how to pour on the charm at just the right time. And soon, he would finally get what he had been wanting since the first day that we met.

A little time had passed between our incident and my mother taking the trip down south to Mississippi. Initially, I asked to go with her. However, she said "no" because there was not enough room for another passenger in the car. Since I couldn't go, I called Mr. Ice to come over that night to spend some time with me. Ironically, right before they were pulling off to head down South, here comes Mr. Ice pulling up. As soon as my mother saw him, she changed her mind and said that I could come along. But, it was too late now. He had already arrived and I wasn't about to leave my company. Besides, my stepfather was still home. Later on while we were down in the basement and my father was probably upstairs asleep, the opportunity presented itself, one thing led to another, and we made love.

When you are caught up in the intensity of intimacy, the farthest thing from your mind are the consequences of having sex. I wanted to enjoy those fleeting moments of sinful pleasure forever. But, God knows, I should have been in that car heading to Mississippi. Instead, I was in my basement losing my virginity. Oh how I enjoyed this aspect of being a women, not knowing that soon after, I would experience another aspect of womanhood. At the age of sixteen, I would become a mother, after having sex for the very first time.

When I found out that I was pregnant, at first I didn't know what to do, or who to tell. At times I was a bundle of mixed emotions. But after I had come to grips with the inevitable, I was excited about being a mother. Most girls my age, particularly at that time, would have been terrified—but, not me.

Many girls in my situation would have considered having an abortion. But, getting rid of my baby was not an option. Of course Mr. Ice had a different opinion about that. But he never pressured me. Soon after that, our relationship went downhill. No matter how hard we tried, the flames of passion between us could not be reignited. Though we tried repeatedly, by the time my son was two years old, I just couldn't try any longer. It was over.

I couldn't keep living the life that Mr. Ice was living. He was no good. He didn't want to work a job. He didn't want to go back to school. We were both parents, with the responsibility to raise our child, but he didn't want to be responsible. He wanted nothing serious out of life. So, eventually he completely defaulted into the life that he knew best and became a common no good thug. Even though he tried to keep it from me, I would hear about him robbing people and sticking up grocery stores.

On one occasion he stuck some man up and even took the shoes off his feet. I went straight to my stepfather and said, "Do I have to be bothered with this man just because I have a baby by him?" My stepfather told me, "No, you don't." And then he reminded me what he said in the beginning when I first started seeing him. My stepfather said "I told you that this man was never going to amount to be anything!" God, how I wished I had listened to his wisdom. My stepfather was certainly right. Today, Ice is in the penitentiary. He's been there since I was twenty-three years old, and is still there today. But we did end up with a beautiful son out of the relationship.

Ice's parents were really awesome when it came down to helping me raise my son. They were there every step of the way and I thank God for them. They took on most of the responsibility. I was still young, running here and there. But they were truly there for me and for my son. They passed away, but lived long enough to see my son grow up and turn out to be the man that he is today.

My son was nine years old when his father went away. My son is now thirty-two and Ice is still trying to call shots, trying to tell my son how to live his life. What nerve! My son is not trying to hear anything his father has to say because of his own bad choices, he lost the right to be my son's advisor.

Sometimes I wonder would Ice have turned out to be a greater man than he became if I would have stayed with him.

When I left Mr. Ice, I never went back for anything; no matter what was promised or what he offered to purchase, when I know the circumstances are not any good for me, I never go back. When I couldn't be bought or persuaded, he switched tactics and started bringing other women around. He thought that by doing that, jealousy would get the best of me. He would also bring those tramps around when he had my son. But that didn't work either, because when I put my mind to something, I stick to it.

Though I never went back to Mr. Ice, I did go back to high school. I was able to go to the prom and most of all I received my high school diploma. Fortunately, I did not lose out on all my teenage years trying to be grown too fast. However, I had to leave my parents' home because I didn't want to come in at the time they wanted me to come in. I ended up moving with Mr. Ice's mother for a little while. I couldn't do anything to satisfy her, so I moved from house to house, living here and there with friends.

Before Ice went to the penitentiary, he did get a chance to meet the other two hustlers that I would eventually be with. He didn't care for either of them. He even threatened them and let them know what he would do to them that if they mistreated his son or did anything out of the norm to his son. My son didn't have any trouble from either hustler.

When I look back over my life, I wish I would have listened more to my children because they may not have all the experience that I did, but they did have insight. Kids can tell you important things, but so often we don't pay them any attention. For example, my son did not like any man that I was in a relationship with. He thought he was my protector. Whenever I would introduce him to a man he'd say, "Uh-uh, no momma, I don't like him. Something's wrong with him." I would just shrug it off as him not liking anybody anyway.

But in 20/20 hindsight, I wish I would have listened to him. I probably wouldn't have gone as far down this road of bad relationships as I did. Since I felt so much rejection in my life, I thought I needed to prove my love to others. I had the same problem that so many other young girls and even grown women have today. Some feel that all you have to do is prove your love and that will change that person into the man you want them to be. But not only does that not work, it's silly to think you can change someone else's heart.

How I thought that I could change someone like Mr. Ice, I don't know. Ice was the way he was because of his upbringing. Number one, he was spoiled and was use to being catered too. Secondly, he was good looking and became vain in his heart. His mother was half Japanese so he had beautiful interracial features. He had a nice light brown skinned complexion and jet black curly hair that laid down his back. He always dressed the part and you would always find him smelling good and well groomed. All the girls wanted him. He lived in a two-flat apartment which his parents owned. They were what we called "hood-rich," which meant that they were doing better than most in a poor neighborhood, but a long way from being rich.

Mr. Ice attended an expensive Catholic high school named Mendel. However, even though he cut classes all the time his parents continued covering for him and even paid his tuition until he finally was kicked out. Though it was clear he was headed for trouble, he never received any consequences to help him straighten up. As far as his parents were concerned, he could do no wrong, neither was anything too good for him.

Mr. Ice grew up with an air of entitlement as if the world owed him something. He walked with a certain swagger of confidence. Even at the age of seventeen he felt he was a big shot, and in charge. Ice got everything he wanted and not just from his parents, but whatever he could take from the streets. He was the type that no one said no to. If they did, he would find a way to get it anyway. His lust for wealth and power always pushed him to get more. For him, there wasn't enough money in working a regular job, so he increased his income by gambling.

Even with all of his vices, he actually was a talented young man. Mr. Ice could really dance, so well in fact, he made a lot of money winning dance competitions. But, contest money wasn't enough for him. His hunger and greed for more got the best of him. So he turned his talents to the streets; drug dealing, credit card fraud, and strong arm robbery. He robbed people for their gym shoes, wallets, drugs, or whatever they had that he might want. Ice even began robbing Currency Exchanges and liquor stores. I never understood why he sunk to such a low level of thuggery when he made plenty of money selling marijuana by the pound. It seemed as if he felt he always had to assert himself because he was short in stature. And maybe he was really driven by a deep seated complex about being short. That's why he always loved driving big cars. Maybe not being able to deal with being a short man, he over compensated with an inflated ego to make himself out to be a big man. Anything that was going to make him look big such as, a big car like a Fleetwood or a Town Car, was his way of being a big man.

Be Wise: Benefit from My Mistakes

Let this be a lesson to all you young ladies out there who like me thought that all that glitters is gold. Trust me, there's more to it than what meets the eye. Years ago there was a popular song out that said, "What you see is what you get."

Usually, that's the furthest thing from the truth. Why? What you can't see is, really what you get.

In 1 Samuel 16:6-7, the prophet Samuel was sent to Jesse's house to choose the next king of Israel. On his own, Samuel had difficulty identifying the Lord's choice. When Samuel saw David's older brother Eliab, this is what happened, "he looked on Eliab, and said, surely the LORD's anointed is before him." But the Lord's response was "Look not on his countenance, or on the height of his stature; because I have refused him: for the LORD seeth not as man seeth; for man looketh on the outward appearance, but the LORD looketh on the heart."

Being deceived by what we see is the oldest trick in the book. It's what got Eve in trouble in the Garden of Eden. After the serpent convinced Eve to partake in the forbidden fruit, her hesitance was arrested once she "...saw that the tree was good for food, and that it was pleasant to the eyes, and a tree to be desired to make one wise, she took of the fruit thereof, and did eat" (Gen. 3:6). This is a limitation that all people have. We can only see what's on the surface, but God can see everything. This is why it is so important to let God direct you in all you do, particularly when you are choosing a mate.

Chapter 3

ONCE WAS NOT ENOUGH

THE SECOND HUSTLER
MR. SKATER

Every wise woman buildeth her house: but the foolish plucketh it down with her hands.
Proverbs 14:1

After reading all the experiences that I had with Mr. Ice, you would have thought that I would be running in the opposite direction of anyone like him. Unfortunately, I kept looking for the same thing but only in different men. Why was that? What was it that was ingrained so deeply within me that it sent me journeying down a road with so many risky relationships? Well, it's like I said in the first chapter; experience is not the best teacher. I had already experienced one bad relationship, but as you will see, that was not enough. What I have learned is, though you could be looking to do the right thing, if you are on the wrong road chances are you still may end up in the wrong place.

One day I made acquaintances with a man in whom I will refer to as Mr. Skater. He happened to notice me because I was all dressed up, out looking for a job. I had obviously caught his eye, so he politely asked my name and what I was doing. I told him I was looking for a job. He then asked me what type of work I was looking for. At that time, I was enrolled in a business college taking up dictation and shorthand. He smiled and then said well this is your lucky day, that he just so happened to know someone looking for a good secretary. He then asked me "How many words per minute do you type?" I told him about 90 words per minute. "Hmm, not bad, let me call my associate and let's see if he still has that opening available," he replied. I was happy about the possibility of getting hired. I had a child to support and I wanted to get on with my life. As well intentioned as I was, Mr. Skater actually had a hidden agenda. The associate that he claimed had the secretarial position was actually in cahoots with Mr. Skater. I had unwittingly fallen into another trap. They were scheming me. Mr. Skater used this game to pick up women.

What was really happening is, his associate, actually his friend, worked at a hospital. So he would answer the phone when I called. I made an appointment and he gave me a time to come. I didn't know that I had been conned until weeks later. Needless to say, I never got the job because there never was a job opening in the first place. That was his way of hustling me.

Once again, my weakness for good looking men betrayed me. Mr. Skater had a fair complexion, was about six feet tall, and was very attractive. He wore a short manicured afro or sometimes his hair would be slicked back like it was permed.

Mr. Skater was from a large family. He had ten other siblings, one which was his twin sister. There was no father figure in his life and after his mother died they were raised by his grandmother. But, just like in his family, since his grandmother wasn't married, there was also no father figure. By the time Mr. Skater had reached the age of ten, his grandmother was too old to adequately raise them. So, at the age of ten Mr. Skater was raising himself. Because of this, he was cast into the role of a parental-child. He had to help raise his siblings and he enjoyed the sense of responsibility. Due to these circumstances, he grew up being a kind hearted man who took care of anyone he considered family. And he faithfully cared for his grandmother until the day she died.

By now, you may be wondering why I call him Mr. Skater. It's simple. He loved to skate and he was a very good skater. Those around the skating rinks, as well as his friends gave him the nickname, Cowboy. Why? Because he wore leather pants with fringes on the side, with the matching leather jacket and matching shirt. He had them in all different colors, ranging from red to black. He had a tailor from the north side custom make all his cowboy clothes. Cowboy seemed harmless enough at first, but there were similarities between him and Mr. Ice, although he was not the textbook hustler. I believe Mr. Skater thought he was a cowboy. However, he wasn't roaming the wild, wild, west; his territory was the wild streets of Chicago.

When we first met, he was only a low-level worker in the drug trade. However, his ambitions were to be a kingpin. In order for him to get promoted to the next level, he had to sell more drugs than anyone else in the house. The house was usually an apartment or single family home that was rented by the head drug dealer who was almost always a gang-banger. Being a successful drug dealer had its perks. Besides the money, there were also a lot of women. The number of women as he had, determined how much harder he had to work to support them. Sometimes business slowed down when the drugs were not flowing from the source. He would be forced to sell his jewelry to get money so he could make ends meet.

He eventually made it to the big time. Just as Mary Kay, gave cars to their top representatives, he too, was given the leader's car. It was a silver Cadillac Seville with a wheel on the back. He was a loyal soldier to the head gang leader, who was the now deceased godfather of the Low End of Chicago. Mr. Skater was such a productive and loyal worker, that the Godfather put him in charge of two high-rise project buildings on 51st Street and 58th Street. This was known as "the hole," which was one of the biggest drug locations in Chicago.

Beside his desire to be a drug kingpin, Mr. Skater also loved to gamble. Whether it was shooting pool or taking people's money in three-card-Molly, he loved the art of the hustle. There were times when he would wear his brother's security guard uniform to impersonate a police officer just to set up people. Pretending to be making an arrest, he would take their drugs and their money. At other times he would stay out for weeks on end casing peoples' homes, noting what time they left home and returned, so he could burglarize them.

Ironically, these were the types of men that I was attracted to. I was never with a man who worked a regular job. And even if a man who had a job did approach me, I didn't want him because I was attracted to fast money making men; thieves, thugs, and criminals. The real question is why? What was it operating in me that kept seeing these types of no good men, as suitable candidates for companionship? Something was amiss in my own heart. All these men were already who they were before I came to them. The issue is, why did I want them? Why did I feel that these men could fill the empty space within my heart? For years, this was a mystery to me.

While I was with Mr. Skater, he too was very protective of me. He never wanted me to be on the bus stop by myself late at night. So, whenever, Mr. Skater wasn't available to come pick me up from work, he would send his friend, (the one who pretended like he had a job for me). His friend had picked me up any number of times, but usually when I got off work late at night. I don't know what Mr. Skater was doing that he couldn't come pick me up himself—probably whoring around with some woman, or involved with one of his criminal activities—he would send his friend. But the last time his friend picked me up; he said something that caught me off guard. He said "Carrie, I can't pick you up any more."

I was wondering, "Why is that?"

He said, "Because I'm starting to get attached to you and I don't want me and you to get any kind of feelings, because I really like my boy and I don't want to do that to him."

But I let him off easy and replied, "What makes you think I want you?" We laughed about it and I understood what he was saying, but he never mentioned it again.

Mr. Skater was good at spoiling me, but he never really taught me anything. He just gave me what he could just to keep me satisfied, while at the same time, giving me heartaches and plenty headaches. Hustlers like Mr. Skater who spend their whole life in pursuit of the almighty dollar, mistakenly think that they can buy things to make you happy. They never seem to understand, that money and material things cannot bring happiness, only the Lord can give you peace and joy.

Mr. Skater was a cheat. He cheated on me with so many women. It's a wonder that I don't have AIDS today, considering the number of women he cheated with. He would go skate at big skating parties, and not invite me. He wanted me to stay at home with his grandmother, which I did. It was like he always wanted to so-call "protect" me. I didn't know why I always needed so much protection; I just wanted to hang out with him. But that was how he would get me out of the way so he could do his dirt.

One particular time, he went skating and told me he would be back home about one or two o'clock in the morning. However, when he hadn't arrived by daybreak, it was a problem. I was the type of person that would call and page him until he answered. That particular day, he wouldn't answer my call, so I got up and drove past every hotel that was on King Drive. He had a fancy car that was easy to spot. Finally, I spotted it in the parking lot of Robert's Motel. Since I had a set of car keys, I hit the panic button and caused the horn to start blowing. This obviously disturbed all of the residents. People were curious and started coming out of their hotel rooms and peeking out the windows because they didn't know who that was out there blowing. Some were scared because it could have been for them. Even with all of that commotion, Mr. Skater, never came to check on his car. Well I wasn't finished. I started yelling, "I know you're in there. By the time I get home, you'd better be at home."

So, not long after I returned home, here comes Mr. Skater, with a tall tale. According to him, it was not him, but that he was letting his boy use his car. He was out gambling all night at the pool hall. He got away by the skin of his teeth on that one because I hadn't checked the pool hall. But alibi or not, I knew he was lying.

When Mr. Skater wouldn't come home at night, he would go get my son from my mother's house. I don't know what he told my mother, but he would come back with my son and my niece. He knew I wouldn't want to act up in front of them. I would just grab my son and my niece, and give them some good ole' sugar because my son was a beautiful boy and my niece was just a little Gerber baby with one piece of hair sticking up in the top of her head. He knew that I loved them and then he would say, "Get dressed. We're going to take them to the zoo." Or we'd take them somewhere to get my mind off of what he did wrong. But I'd whisper to him, "I'm going to get you later."

If it wasn't Mr. Skater's antics that I had to put up with, it was the other women who wanted him. This one particular woman wanted him so bad that she tried to set me up. It all occurred when I was working at a gas station. She sent this man to the gas station. I didn't know she was actually hiding behind the gas station. She thought that since this man was really nice looking, that I was going to fall for him and start cheating on Mr. Skater.

So, he came up to the gas station, calling himself rapping to me. I must admit he was nice looking and everything. But the problem was this brother's hair was longer than mine. I told him, "I don't mess with men whose hair is longer than mine."

He told me, "I'm going to get you, if it takes five years from now."

So, he went on and on for about fifteen or twenty minutes. But I still never took the bait. I found out later that this jealous sister was behind the whole thing. She wanted to go back and tell Mr. Skater that I was cheating on him or that I took this brother's number, so we could fall out and then she could take my place. But that didn't work. She didn't know that I took care of his grandmother when he wasn't around. I needed a place to live and didn't want to go back home.

I found out later that the sister who tried to set me up at the gas station lived on Damen. My mother lived one block over and maybe five blocks down. That's why Mr. Skater would always be able to get my son so quickly, because the sister he was cheating with lived close by. The problem was that she wasn't just a chick on the side, he really did like her.

One night I got off work late and called his pager to see if he could pick me up. He never answered. It was about one o'clock in the morning. I was working at the Amoco gas station at the time. So a friend happened to pull up for some gas and I asked, "Can you drop me off down the street? It's too late for me to walk." As soon as I grabbed the guy's car door, Mr. Skater came flying up on us. He scared me to death. Once he got out of the car, I could see the rage in his eyes. I told him, "It was too dangerous for me to walk. I called you numerous times and you didn't answer the phone. You didn't call me back. I didn't want to walk, and this guy just so happened to pull up." Of course, he didn't believe me. After that day, he made sure he wasn't too busy to take me home. He made sure I didn't want for anything. And when he picked me up from work and dropped me at home, he'd make sure I got in safely and keep on going.

With him being gone so much and me staying at the family home, I became his grandmother's caretaker. I also took care of his great aunt who was in her eighties. I would see after both of them when I got off of work. I'd help them out around the house, cleaning up a little and fixing their meals. Whatever they needed, I faithfully did it for them. Mr. Skater began to get so comfortable knowing that I was there with his grandmother. If I was there taking care of them, meant I wasn't out there cheating on him. He was obviously haunted by his own guilty conscience—to a cheater, everybody cheats.

By this time, I was nineteen or twenty but I wasn't the type that went to lounges to hang out. However, I never wanted to go back home. So I was living wherever I could. But, I never slept on the streets or in the park or anything like that. I was fortunate because someone would always take me in. Mr. Skater happened to be one of those that did. Initially, he was good to me and we became lovers. We had an intense intimate relationship, to such a degree, Mr. Skater believed that I was head-over-heels about him, that I would be around forever. But after a while I just got tired of that.

During this time I happened to run into an old girlfriend of mine. We began to talk about what was going on in my life. It was so good to be able to share my feelings with some-one outside of Mr. Skater's associates. I let her know about my situation and that I didn't want to deal with him any-more. My friend offered to let me stay with her for a while. So I packed the few clothes I had and moved in with her. One night my girlfriend picked me up from work and as we pulled into her driveway, Mr. Skater was already there waiting for us. Unbeknown to us, he must have followed me home one night. That was the kind of person he was, lurking in the darkness.

As soon as we pulled into the driveway, he jumped out of the car like he was a crazy man. I was terrified, but my friend wasn't having it. How dare he trespass on her property? She immediately told him that if he didn't get off her property she was calling the police. Even though he left, he wasn't finished harassing me.

On another occasion my girlfriend and I went out to a nightclub called Studio 79. We had prearranged for her sister to pick us up afterwards. At 1:00 her sister still hadn't shown up. So we had no choice but to wait for her on this cool fall night. However, her sister never showed. Fortunately, the owner of Studio 79 saw us still standing outside as he was locking up. So he offered to take us home. Once again, Mr. Skater was hiding down the street from where I was living. We pulled up, and as soon as I got out the car, he came flying down the street in his car. It scared the daylights out of me. He grabbed me and threw me in the car so hard that I hit my side on the steering wheel. My friend was screaming my name and she ran in the house to call the police. But he took off with me and made a clean getaway. In just a few minutes, Mr. Skater took me to an abandoned building not too far from where he abducted me. I thought I was going to die. But once we got into the building all he wanted to do was tell me how much he loved me. I was so relieved that he didn't want to hurt me, but there was no way I was ever going back to be with him. I was fed up with that life.

While I was with Mr. Skater, I didn't do much partying. However, my friend that I moved in with was into the night life. She was a party girl. So once I started hanging out at clubs, I changed my appearance and I changed my attitude. Now all I wanted to do every weekend was to go out and party. But come to find out that Mr. Skater was still stalking me. He would hide and follow us to every party that we went to. This last particular party, he came up on me and tried to take my jewelry (a diamond ring, a gold necklace, and bracelets), that he bought for me. My girlfriend looked at me and said,

"Look, do you want him?"

"No, I don't want him," I emphatically replied.

"Well give him back his stuff. Give it all to him."

I gladly took off everything that I had that belonged to him. I was through with his tail for good. I guess he didn't think I was going to respond that way. He thought by demanding back the jewelry he had given me that I would come back to him. Well he had another thing coming because diamonds were not this girl's best friend. I didn't care about him or that jewelry. And that was the last time I had a face to face interaction with him. But that wasn't the last time that he stalked me.

Me and my girlfriend didn't come home right after the party that night. Instead, we went to an all-night card game. When we did come home, it was past twelve o'clock the next afternoon. And guess who was in the driveway again—Mr. Skater. This time, something was on his mind. He didn't seem his usual suspicious self. I could tell something was bothering him. Though he didn't tell me then, his grandmother had just passed away. Part of him wanted to tell me, the other part didn't want to break the bad news. However, later on that night, I had to find out from his best friend that his grandmother had died.

Then I understood why he acted so strange when he was there waiting on me. He was conflicted over being hurt about the death of his grandmother, but more upset with me. In his jealous mind Mr. Skater was angry with me, because he thought that I had been out with another man. But that wasn't true. We were just out having a good time. Besides, I was no longer attached to him, and I was enjoying my freedom. To be honest, I really wasn't looking to get in anymore close relationships anyway. I needed a break from all that. I was enjoying my singleness and not having any relationship accountability. But he was behaving like we were still together. It was like he was having a nervous breakdown after I left him.

A couple days after his grandmother's death, I found out about the funeral arrangements. Since I was so close to his grandmother, of course I attended the funeral. The day of the funeral, his sister, and his auntie rode together in the family car. The young lady from the gas station was at the funeral also. I could tell that she had an attitude as soon as she saw I was at the funeral with the family. She completely blew her top and took a brick and threw it at the car just because I was in there. Mr. Skater must have told her that his family really loved me because I helped take care of his grandmother. After it was all over, I'm sure that she was feeling really stupid about what she did, particularly considering the history that I had with the family. I had more right to be there then she did. But she gave into a jealous rage and ended up embarrassing herself. It was actually amusing watching her make a fool of herself, particularly since at that point Mr. Skater and I were no longer together.

After the burial I returned back to his auntie's house for the repast. Not long after we arrived there, he came storming in, asking why I came to the funeral. He told me I needed to stay away from them. By this, I knew then that he was in love with her. I told him, "Look, all the crazy stuff you did like stalking me everywhere. I didn't come here today because I'm stalking you. And I don't care about you being with her. I just came to support the family."

His complaint was that I was messing up his current relationship. But he hadn't considered that he had already messed up my life after breaking my heart. He had me thinking that he was this great person and we were going to live happily ever after, and all the time he was cheating. The same woman that was trying to hook me up at the gas station is who he ended up with. They also had a child together.

But ten years down the line, Mr. Skater would still try to find out how I was doing and one day he found me. I was working at a shop, and in walked Mr. Skater. He came over to me and said, "Just wanted to say hello, see how you were doing, and if you needed anything."

I quickly responded, "No, thank you." I had no interest in him at all.

Back when I was living with my girlfriend and we thought Mr. Skater had faded out for a little while, we began going to different places and having club sets. I also began waiting tables at the club sets because I was good with people. That was part of my commitment for our club sets. I had no problem waiting tables. I always came home with the most tips. We decided to have our last club set at a different location than where we usually had it. It was a little spot in the neighborhood called Sandy's.

As I walked into the club, there was a telephone booth right near the entrance. I noticed this man talking on the telephone. As I walked by him, he grabbed my hand. I let him hold it for a second, and then I pulled it away gently. Later that night he came up to me, and asked me if he could have my number. "Yeah, you can have it," I replied. So we exchanged numbers and soon afterwards, I left. At the time, I was not in a serious relationship with anyone, although there were a couple of guys that I was flirting around with. I never called this guy, but a few days later he decided to call me.

He asked me to go out on a date and I told that would be fine. On the way back from our date, I saw this young man that I knew who lived in the neighborhood. He was standing on the bus stop. I asked him if he could drop the brother off. That's the kind of person I was, and still am today. He let the brother in, but to my surprise the brother we picked up, tried to act like there was something going on between him and I. I was shocked by the way he was playing it, especially since it wasn't true. My date was very upset. So, after we dropped the guy off he turned and slapped me for asking him to give a ride to another man that I was dating. But, it wasn't true. But now that wasn't the issue. He had just put his hands on me and I was not the one for that. Now, he had another problem altogether.

We got in front of my girlfriend's house. I jumped out of that car and went in the house looking for a butcher knife or something, but by the time I got back outside he was gone. I should have left him then, but I didn't. I entered this relationship as a way of erasing Mr. Skater out my mind. That's the reason I let the brother take me out again. He was a little better. As weeks went by, we started talking about things. He had a ready-made family. I never had a man that had a ready-made family. He had two kids and a lot of baby's momma drama, but he still brought me around his family. This was a little intimidating because I never had to knowingly compete with another women. I had always been the one or the only one, or so I thought. But this situation was a little different.

As we began to get to know one another better we began to share about our lives and our backgrounds. That's when I found out something about him that blew me away. As I mentioned earlier in this chapter, there was a situation where the woman who Mr. Skater was cheating on me with, tried to set me up with a good looking man with long hair while I was working at the gas station. It was that guy that I told, "that I would not date a man that had longer hair than me." And then he said, "if it takes him five years he was going to get me." Well come to find out, this was the same man. I didn't recognize him because he had cut off all his hair, and did not look the same. Besides that, I only saw him that one time anyway. He already knew who I was at the club the night I walked by him and he grabbed my hand. He already knew my name before I told him my name. He never told me until months later that he was that same man.

Chapter 4

"For a just man falleth seven times, and
riseth up again…"
Proverbs 24:16

MR. RUTHLESS

It's amazing. Some of the trials and tribulations we experience in life are from things we bring upon ourselves. The question that has baffled me and others is, why do people keep going back to the things that are no good for them? Why would a women that has been abused by one man, end up in a relationship with another abusive man? Though the dynamics of why people do the things that they do is a complex issue, the answer is actually simple. People do, or get involved in things and relationships that are normal to them. Then what's normal to them becomes their "natural." So, a person who is raised in chaos, their normal is coping with chaos, and they naturally gravitate towards things, situations, and even people where chaos and instability are present. People can only do what they know. This is why the Bible admonishes us to be "transformed by the renewing of our mind," so we will discover what God's perfect will for our life is. Trust me, God's plan is better than our plan.

One would think that after Mr. Ice and Mr. Skater, that I would have had enough negative experiences dealing with hustlers, that I would be running in the opposite direction. But I didn't run. I hopped from the frying pan into the skillet.

I liken my situation to a person treading water in a swimming pool. After a while they want to get out of the water. The only problem is, the ladder to climb out of the pool, is in deeper water than what they are currently in. So they have to go into deeper water to get out. Before they know it, they're in deeper waters, and in over their head.

As for me, I still hadn't learned my lesson yet so once again I got involved with another hustler. But this time, the man I was involved with was not a wanna-be-hustler; he was the real deal, the "alpha male." An alpha male is the dominant male of a group. He is the leader, the strongest and the baddest. He's the one who others are afraid to challenge, and the one who demands respect, and will assert his dominance to the degree of killing any challengers. That's who I ended up with, the alpha male who I call Mr. Ruthless.

Mr. Ruthless like the others came from a big family. He was the youngest of nine, but the way his mother talked about him, you would have thought he was the only child. This hustler could do no wrong in her eyes. That was her baby. He was a muscular man standing about six-feet-two, with a pretty caramel color complexion. He also had big beautiful brown eyes, and when I first met him, long silky hair. To look at him you would have never imagined that Mr. Ruthless was a serious gang-banger, but he was. Everybody who knew him, also knew he didn't play. His nickname in the street was Magilla Gorilla, because he thought nothing about going ape on somebody.

Mr. Ruthless had bodyguards who went everywhere with him. He started hustling at age fifteen and was a father by the same age. With a criminally enterprising mind, his drug of choice was cocaine, or as they called it in back in those days, "White Girl." Don't get me wrong, he didn't turn down anything that could make him a profit. But his eyes were on the big dollars that cocaine trafficking could bring. Though most of what he did was illegal, he was very smart and a successful businessman.

Unlike the average hustler, Mr. Ruthless possessed legitimate credentials; he was a licensed cosmetologist. But the money he made doing hair, wasn't enough for him. At that time, I was in beauty school and he had his own beauty shop. He asked if I would work at his beauty shop. I agreed and became his shampoo girl. While he should have focused on hair, his mind was on drugs. There were times I would shampoo the young ladies to have them ready for his arrival but he would never show up. So I started doing their hair. They didn't like the way I did their hair because they wanted him. They didn't want me to shampoo. They only wanted him. So all his clients began to fade away and I began picking up my own clientele from those who walked in or liked how I did hair—they became my regulars. That's how I got into the hair business.

One day, Mr. Ruthless and I were talking about events in my past, and I told him of some of the changes that I had gone through with Mr. Skater. That's all it was at first with Mr. Ruthless just work and good conversations. One day Mr. Ruthless came over to the house where I lived and he asked,

"Is it alright for me to come here? I know you're living with other people and everything."

"Yes, it's fine," I responded.

"Can I take off my shoes," he kindly asked?

I said, "Sure, you can take off your shoes." So he stepped into our little den area where we entertained our guests. Suddenly, there was a knock at the door not even three minutes after he walked in. And I heard Mr. Skater's voice. "What are you doing at this door?" I said through the door.

"Open up this door!"

"I'm not opening up this door. What are you here for?" I replied.

Mr. Ruthless said, "Go ahead open up the door for him."

I opened the door, and in walks Mr. Skater acting like we were still together. Then in a sudden fit of rage he picked up a chair, as if he was going to hit me. Mr. Ruthless told him, "If you hit her with that chair, I will beat you like you stole something. This is my woman now. She already told me that you had been stalking her. I want you to know that this is my woman now and I had better not catch you anywhere near her ever again." Of course Mr. Skater stopped dead in

58

his tracks, because he didn't want any part of Mr. Ruthless. After that, Mr. Skater never came around me again.

As time went on, we became very close to one another. We had a very tight bond. I received his undivided attention. It was like there was no other woman around, even though I knew that this was not true. He had another family. But whenever I was around him it was just him and I.

Approximately one year into our relationship, I ended up getting pregnant by him. When I told him that I was pregnant, he didn't want the baby. He gave me a hundred and fifty dollars and told me to go have an abortion. I told his mother about it, and she told me not to get rid of her grandbaby. However, I went on down to the abortion clinic anyway.

The clinic was on Michigan Avenue. I got there, got fully undressed, and as I was putting on the gown, I heard a still small voice in the room with me that said, "Carrie, get out of there." Nobody was in the room but me. The nurse had gone out of the room so I could get undressed and said she would be right back. But after hearing that voice (which I now know was the Lord) I put on my clothes darted out of that office, and went running down Michigan Avenue. I ran like I had just stole something.

I could not get rid of my baby. Not knowing who else to call, I called his mother, and asked her to come pick me up. Since I still had the one-hundred and fifty dollars, I gave his mother some of it for coming to get me from the 'L' Station.

Now he had started getting real nervous about me being pregnant and he really didn't know what to do. We were both young. He was twenty at the time and I was twenty-one. But age didn't matter now, because what was done, was done. So, he really started to appease me by buying me things, and reassuring me by saying I was the only one in his life right now. He would buy me perfume and give me jewelry. He ended up giving me the first apartment of my own. I was so excited that I didn't have to live with anybody else! I had my own little place. And everything that he bought for me was quality merchandise; nothing he gave me was cheap. Showering me with gifts was the way he used to keep reeling me back in. The more I took from him the deeper into his world I sunk.

Soon, he started getting real big in the drug game. I began to get scared and wanted to run. He wouldn't let me. We started fighting more. He said he would kill me if I left him. Now women from every race were coming from all directions. He began to get greedy and I began to get fat. I was all out of proportion. I told him, "This is not what I signed up for." As we use to say, everything started getting out of whack.

He said that I knew too much to leave him and he wasn't going to just let me go. He began to try to teach me how to bag up cocaine, how to bag up weed. He taught me how to start weighing up cocaine. It was like I was one of his workers. He started trusting me with the money. We began to make so much money, it was unbelievable. I knew what I was doing was wrong and I felt guilty about it. But I suppressed those feelings and kept doing it anyway.

As I was learning more about the drug business, our love for each other started to fade. We became more like partners than lovers. He wasn't looking as fine as he was when I first met him. But the cash was looking real good, so I stayed even longer. I took advantage of the situation and went back to cosmetology school. I earned my certificate and got my license. But, Mr. Ruthless' mind was always on his drug empire. That's the business he wanted me to learn. He said, "This is the reason I'm teaching you these things, so if something ever happens to me, you will know how to take care of yourself." But that was the bright side of the coin. He wasn't telling me that I could end up dead or in the penitentiary. However, as he began to realize that my heart really wasn't in the drug game like his was, he started becoming critical of me and called me a dummy because I'd rather earn my money the honest way. That really frustrated him.

At one point he said he was going to stop coming around me because I always had something negative to say. My positive things were his negative things. We were so polarized it's like we no longer spoke the same language. I really didn't have negative things to say. I was just being honest about this life and the ugly things he was exposing me to. None of my prior relationships had ever brought me this deeply into the game as Mr. Ruthless had.

However, once I received my cosmetology license, he became so jealous. This meant that I was able to be independent and strike out on my own. He started pointing his finger all in my face, saying, "You think you something 'cause you got a license and everything. I hope you ain't planning on leaving me." However, he was just succumbing to his own sense of insecurity. I wasn't ready to leave him, not yet anyway, because I was still working on getting myself together. But as always, I wanted to do what Carrie wanted to do. I wanted to do Carrie's life and not his life. The cocaine game was the life that he chose. But something was calling me away from that life. I was now being called to follow a straight and narrow path.

A CHANGE SOON TO COME

One day my older sister invited me to come to her church. By that time, I had already had my daughter, my second child. I was glad that my sister had invited me to church, but it was mainly because I wanted God to save Mr. Ruthless. The way I saw it, he was the one that needed fix'n. Unfortunately, my request to come to church fell upon death ears—he wasn't ready. However, later on I decided to get my daughter christened and I insisted that he come. As usual he didn't want to go anywhere near a church, no matter what the reason. As a matter of fact, he even tried to offer to take me out to dinner, so he wouldn't have to come to the christening. I told him, look, I can eat dinner anywhere any time, but a baby christening is a once in a life time event. Eventually, he felt convicted and finally decided to come. I was grateful to God that he was there to witness his daughter being dedicated to the Lord.

After the christening, I continued attending church and I started developing a closer relationship with the Lord. Apparently, there was an obvious change in my life and it started to bother Mr. Ruthless' spirit because everything about me started to change. The lifestyle changes I was making started to get under his skin. He used to complain saying, "Now all you do is talk about all this Jesus stuff." He couldn't stand being in my presence. My language began to change for the better. He said he didn't want to come around me anymore because I was talking negative to him. No, I wasn't talking negative; I was trying to help him get out of the gangster life. I was trying to let him know there was a better life. I told him that I wasn't speaking negative. It was just that we weren't speaking the same language anymore. I was speaking things that pertained to the kingdom of God, and he was speaking things pertaining to the kingdom of darkness.

Yet despite our differences, I stayed in the relationship with him. Oddly, the more I attended that Baptist church, the bigger Mr. Ruthless became in the drug underworld. In fact, they named him one of the drug kingpins citywide; from the north side, east side, west side, and south side. All while this was happening, I was going to church, but I wasn't saved yet. I had not yet been born again and baptized with the Holy Ghost. Basically, I still had one foot in the world and one foot in the church. But by me attending more often, the idea of living right really started to have an impact on me. But I still had not fully surrendered to the Lord, nor was I committed to the church. My flesh still had too much authority over my actions and desires.

One of the things that I have always liked to do was dance; so I started stepping. I really liked to step and I felt that stepping was okay, so I went to a lot of stepping parties. I obviously felt that fornicating was okay too. Besides, the preacher at the church I was attending never preached against sin. When I went to services at that church, there was no conviction at all so I thought fornicating, adultery, lying, partying and all that were okay too. So I was still in the world and outside of God's perfect will for my life. Therefore, the devil took advantage of my inconsistency and tried to pull me in deeper before I could escape to the safety of salvation.

As for Mr. Ruthless, he continued to excel in the drug world. By the time our daughter was two years old, he said, "I don't want you to live in an apartment any more. I want you to look for a house." When he said that, two things happened, I got excited as well as distracted. Here I was only twenty-five years old and I was about to move into my own home.

Once I got all settled into my new home, the enemy tried to dig his claws deeper into me. Whereas the other two hustlers kept me away from their illegal enterprises, now Mr. Ruthless was getting me directly involved in the drug trade. He first started teaching me how to sell the drugs, and how to build up a network of sellers. So I reached out to those I felt I could trust and convinced to join in with me. I reached out to some of my own family members. I had one of my cousins as a runner. I had my brother helping out as well. I mean, I had it all planned. But there was one thing that I hadn't calculated in my sinful equation, and that was the possibility that some of the family members that I brought into the drug game, could get turned out on dope themselves. To this day, I regret that. When I look back on it, we all thought that we were in the mix, having some good times while making some money. But the truth was all I really did was introduce destruction to my family.

Yes, I had the house and all the other things that a young woman could want. But deep down on the inside, I wasn't happy. I was still considered as his woman, even though he had other women at the time when he bought my house. I was thinking that I was "all that" and that I was his special one, until I found out that he bought two other sisters houses too. That was hard to deal with because he was crazy enough to buy our homes in the same vicinity. Just walking down the street, we were liable to trip over one another. We all lived five minutes from each other. I use to wonder how he could get home so quickly when he claimed that he was somewhere else far away.

Sometimes he would come to my house for breakfast. On those occasions when he was there, I tried not to upset him by confronting him about his whereabouts. I wanted him to spend time with our daughter. She would always ask him if he would spend the night. He would always have an excuse why he couldn't spend the night or stay. It would always disappoint my baby that daddy wouldn't stay.

One of the other people he bought a house for was his mother. She had a nice big old five-bedroom house. He told me that he would be living with his mother, so if I wanted or needed him, that's where he would be. So one particular time she called my house asking if he was there. I said, "No. I talked to him last night and he said he was spending the night with you."

She said, "Well, he's not here. I haven't seen him and I have not even talked to him."

That was a red flag. In a roundabout way she was letting me know that he had not been at her house. But I had a feeling that he was going to be calling me. Pretty soon, he did. When the phone rang, I knew it was him. With an attitude I asked "Where are you? Where have you been?" "I told you I was gonna be staying with my momma," he replied.

I said, "Your momma called here this morning and she said she hadn't seen or talked to you all night long." (When she would get mad at him, that's when she would start telling on him). Mr. Ruthless knew I had a temper and that I would fight him. Even though he was six feet tall, and meaner than a junk yard dog, I didn't care. I would still fight him. I got in his face and told him; "If I'm going to be your woman, I'm going to be your woman. I'm not going to share you with those other women you have. Bring all of them here, and we'll sit down at the table and let's have a sister-to-sister discussion about whose man you really are. Let's have a family affair. If you're going to be a player, then be a player, but you are not going to keep playing me!" He called my bluff and said he was going to call them, but of course he didn't. All I wanted him to do was be for real and put it all out there on the table.

But he couldn't and didn't know how to deal with me confronting him like that. It caught him off guard, because he was accustomed to everyone bowing down to him. I was fed up. I said, "Forget this, I'm just going to go ahead and leave." When I said I'm leaving, then I knew there was going to be a fight just like it had been in the past when I'd threatened to do it.

I remember one time when him and I were at it, I just jumped in my car, and drove to my auntie's house. He had the nerve to bust into her house with his gun out. It didn't faze my auntie one bit. She got her gun and said "listen here; you ain't the only one with a gun." She put her gun on the table, he put his gun on the table, and he said, "Okay let's you and me talk about this thing." "You want to talk, to my niece but she said she doesn't want to be bothered with you right now. Give it some time for her to cool off, and then she might want to talk to you."

He said, "Well, auntie you tell her, that I took her piggy bank and I took one of every shoe that she has because I know she loves her high heel shoes."

That was just one of the many incidents we have had. I can recall fighting him until I couldn't fight him anymore. He's punched me a couple of times and bruised up my face real bad. But after all of that, I still couldn't break away. I didn't know it or understand it at the time, but it was an ungodly soul tie that I had with him. When you develop an ungodly soul-tie with someone, it is very difficult to just walk away, it's like you are under some type of spell.

But, he was delusional too. He was crazy enough to think that my cousins that worked for him, were going to stand by and let him abuse me. He had another thing coming. They let him know that they didn't care who he was, but told him what they would do to him, if they ever found out he abused me. My family members threatened him, especially my two cousins that were only fifteen and sixteen years old at the time. On one occasion we were at my auntie's house arguing and they came running down the stairs because they heard all the commotion. Trying to sway them to his side he said,

"Man, y'all understand don't cha."

"No we don't understand," they angrily responded. My auntie yelled at them, "Yawl get ready for school!"

"We ain't getting ready for school until he gets out of here," they emphatically insisted.

My auntie was smart. She told him, he had to leave her house right then and there so her sons could get ready to go to school. He left out of there looking so pitiful because he was so accustomed to whipping every woman who ever stood up to him. I knew for a fact that with his other girlfriends he whipped some of everyone in their family. He was that brutal. However, he never got a chance to touch a person in my family because we stuck together. Because of that, he never tried to challenge any of us—only me.

After we had gotten past that situation, only a little time had passed when I ran up on him with a couple other ladies. Of course he denied that there was anything between them. He just said that they were just some girls who were helping him out and working for him. But silly me, I fell for that. Like any kingpin, you must treat your workers right or soon, they will break ranks and turn on you. One lesson he hadn't learned yet is that intimidation will only take you so far. He thought his boys were "his boys"—that they would always have his back. But within the next few days, some of them told on him.

It was just unbelievable the life I have lived with this brother. But I was tired of all the danger and drama. But whenever I could find my way to the house of the Lord, I would be crying out to Him, asking God to help me get away from this life. I would pray, plead, and cry. "God please help me. Please God deliver me from this life. Deliver me from myself. Please God help me!"

It didn't happen right away, but as time passed the love that I had for him began to fade, and that ungodly soul-tie began to unravel. Slowly but surely we started drifting apart from each other. And at a certain point we both understood that we just couldn't be together any longer. We both had too much jealousy and too much rage within us. That was an explosive mixture that had become too dangerous for us both. We were young. We had great potential. But we were on two different roads, headed in two different directions. Each time we tried to meet up at an intersection, we would only end up crashing. So what was the use trying to kid ourselves any longer?

The new year had come and gone. Winter's cold grip had loosed and spring was now upon us. It was Mother's Day. Yes,

I was the mother of two children, but neither of their fathers was around to honor me. Admittedly, I was feeling lonely. I missed a man being in my life. Deep inside me my emotions screamed out for that companionship that I had grown so accustomed to. I missed the intimacy and the intensity of a man that knew how to please me. I was experiencing a period of vulnerability, and the devil was there waiting for me.

My daughter and I were out taking a ride. We decided to stop by my brother's house. When we did, out of nowhere, Mr. Ruthless pulled up. I had on this real pretty green dress. My daughter had on her little two-piece green outfit. He stepped out with a green silk suit on. We were all color coordinated just like a family would be. As soon as I saw him, the devil whispered in my mind saying, "You know that you are supposed to be together." So that particular night he asked if he could come over, and I allowed him to come over. Once he was in my house, I dropped my guard, and my resistance melted away under intense heat of our own lustful passion. That night, I laid with him. But his loving that I thought I so missed was gone in an instant. Because, not ten minutes after we were intimate, he got up, got dressed, and left. Oh God, I felt so cheated. It felt like I had been raped. And that devil who whispered in my ear, enticing me to sin was now laughing at me and calling me a fool.

As soon as he left, I ran to the shower and tried to wash the filth of our fornication off my body. I scrubbed myself as if I had fallen into a cesspool. I wanted the stench of my sin off of me. I wanted the remembrance of his touch washed away from me once and for all. After that Mother's Day night, I never slept with him again.

When I got out of the shower, I went down on my knees and told the Lord that I couldn't do it anymore. I didn't want to live like that anymore. I pleaded with God, I said, "Lord if you aren't going to take me away from this terrible life, at least take this man away from me." After I prayed, I cried myself to sleep, not knowing how I was going to deal with my situation. But the Lord was already working things out.

On June 5th, the Feds came down on him so tough. Everything that he thought he owned, the Feds were there to confiscate. The story of his arrest was covered in the newspapers and on all the local television channels in Chicago. They even came by one of my businesses, asking me all kinds of questions about him. I let them know that I didn't know anything too much about that brother, no more than we had a baby together. I didn't want them to take what I had. I was so glad that we were out of each other's life.

Once all the indictments started coming down, we started going to court. I had to go because I too, was suspected of being a part of his money laundering enterprise. They had me coming down giving samples of my signature to see if I was signing any of those checks. They also had almost our whole family coming down. They finally got him on conspiracy charges, but as for me, God allowed me to escape being prosecuted and going to jail.

I praise God, that He delivered me and allowed me to flee that wicked life. Because, during the time I was dealing with Mr. Ruthless, I think about three or four of our friends had been gunned down and killed.

When the trial was all over, he received fifteen years in the penitentiary, which he had to do thirteen of those years. During those thirteen years, I may have tried to go see him once. But to be honest, I never wanted to waste my gas going back and forth down there to see him. However, he had to settle for calling once a week for thirteen years, checking up on his daughter, when he could have been there with her. But he made the choice and he chose the gangster life over his own family.

In all fairness I'm not trying to disgrace Mr. Ruthless because there were positive aspects of him. He was truly a brilliant young man with great potential. If he would have put his energy into positive pursuits he could have become a successful businessman. He was also a good provider. Anything that I wanted or anything my daughter wanted—from a home, to cars, to furs, to diamonds—we never went without. He was always available when there was a need. But aside from all the material things, what my daughter really needed was a good father figure, to spend quality time with her and love her. But evidentially, there was really no love in him. So, he couldn't give what he never had. In his world, money and material things were god. That's why it was easier to give us things than to give us his love and his heart.

Chapter 5

I Should Have Gone To Jail…
But God!

"It is of the LORD's mercies that we are not consumed, because his compassions fail not. They are new every morning: great is thy faithfulness."
Lamentations 3:22-23

When I was coming up, whenever someone got away with something that they should have gotten in trouble for, we use to say, "You are lucky that you didn't get caught." And usually, that so-called lucky person might respond by emphasizing what it was that they did to evade consequences. Boasting, they may say, "yeah I out smarted them," "I was faster than them," or something of that nature. The fact is, in life there are many times that we do not get the punishment or consequences what we deserve. But let me be clear, it's not because you are lucky. There are no good luck charms that you can wear around your neck to ward off unfavorable circumstances; that's mere superstition. Nevertheless, there were many times that I was spared, but it wasn't because of a rabbit's foot dangling from my neck or some lucky stars lining up in my favor. Clearly, it was the Lord's mercy that I was not consumed.

When my daughter was about three weeks old, I remember Mr. Ruthless had bought me a used Toyota. One day, while on the Dan Ryan Expressway my car stopped. I called and asked him if he could come and pick me up. When he pulled up to get me, he was driving his Lincoln Town Car with dark tinted windows. It was his favorite car that he considered to be his luxury car. Usually, he only drove that car at night. But this particular time, he used it to come get me in the middle of the day.

By this time, I was now running late for work. He pulled up with one of his friends in the car with him. As we got closer to 63rd Street to get off the Expressway, there were some unmarked police cars with detectives in them following us. Next thing I knew, they were pulling us over. I didn't know that he had cocaine on him. So, as soon as they pulled us over, he threw the cocaine over to me. I'm throwing it back at him and he's throwing it back at me. He said, "They ain't gonna search you. Hide it in your panties!" So I did what he said, and he was right, the male officers couldn't search me, but they called a woman detective to come search me. She knew where to look. So now, instead of me heading to work, I was on my way to city lock-up.

When we got to the precinct, they said, "we know that you aren't the drug dealer. We know that the dope we found on you is not yours. We know it's his because we've been watching him for a long time. All we need from you is information. We don't plan on locking you up." But I wasn't about to start talking.

When they saw that this tactic wasn't working on me, they switched game plans. They thought for sure that they could get under my skin by telling about all the other woman that he had. But, I already knew about them and they weren't telling me anything that I didn't know already. Therefore, the tactic to get me to rollover on Mr. Ruthless didn't work. I had nothing to say. They were ticked off, but thanks be to God, they finally let me go.

I could have easily been locked up. The drugs were on me. I could have been charged and my boyfriend could have gone free, and I could have lost custody of my daughter. But God who is rich in mercy stepped in and He set me free.

Another occasion where I escaped being locked up was involving one of Mr. Ruthless' workers. I don't know why, but I never liked this guy. I use to let Mr. Ruthless know that I didn't like this guy. He was like, "What did he do to you? What is it about him that you don't like?"

I said, "I don't know. I can't put my hands on it yet, but there's just something about him." I noticed right away that everything Mr. Ruthless would buy, this guy would also purchase. Everything Mr. Ruthless would wear, he would go get something similar to it. Normally, men don't do that. That's what women usually do. So I knew he had a jealous spirit on him, but at first I didn't know how bad it was.

One particular occasion, the guy borrowed some money from Mr. Ruthless and when he asked the guy for his money back, the guy didn't want to pay him his money back. He told me that the guy had asked him to come down to the projects to meet him. I knew something was wrong, and I told Mr. Ruthless, "Don't go over there. Let him come to you."

But he went anyway. He took one of his friends with him, but his friend didn't go up; he stayed down in the car. So when Mr. Ruthless got up to the top of the stairs, the guy confronted him and said that his woman accused him of try-ing to seduce her. Mr. Ruthless told the man, "Your woman ain't even my type. Why would I do something like that? Man, I just came up here to get my money. That's what y'all need to be getting together, my money."

He said, "Alright man, let's go get your money, after you." So once Mr. Ruthless started walking in front of him, he hit Mr. Ruthless in the back of the head with a pipe, knocking him out cold. By the time he regained consciousness and made it back to my house, I knew something had to be wrong, because he didn't go home he came to my house.

He said, "You told me not to trust this guy, but yet I still did." About a year later he asked me if I would meet this same guy for something. I told him, "No, I can't. I don't like him like that."

He said, "Please, would you do it for me for this last time? I need you to meet this guy for me because I'm somewhere else and I can't get there."

Finally being persuaded, I reluctantly agreed to go and pick up some drugs on Mr. Ruthless' behalf. However, I had to go grocery shopping first. Once I reached my apartment,

I started putting up my groceries, when something strange began to happen. Something inside me started talking to me. (Today I know it was the Holy Spirit.) The Spirit told me to "hide it." Then this sense of urgency came over me. Not really understanding why, I quickly hid the dope. And, a minute after I hid the drugs, there was a loud knock at the door. No one that I knew would knock like that. It was the police. There were about four uniformed officers and four or five narcotics detectives. They came in my house and asked if there were any drugs in my house? Of course I told them, no, I don't have any drugs here. And of course they didn't believe me, so they ransacked my house looking for those drugs.

What they did find was a .22 caliber pistol that I had gotten from my grandfather. So they took me in for that, until they could run it. After they did, they discovered that it was registered so they couldn't hold me for that. They didn't find the cocaine, but they found other things that I shouldn't have had. So, they placed me under arrest, handcuffed me and read me my rights and took me to jail.

I stayed in jail for one day. The next day, Mr. Ruthless made sure he got me the best lawyer there was because he knew how my mother and my family felt about me. The lawyer he retained for me, was a great lawyer. As long as I live I will never forget him.

The attorney told me, "Don't worry, I'm going to get you out of this, the judge is my friend, he and I are going fishing over the weekend and I'm going to talk to him about your case." He also gave me this solemn warning, "If you do not leave this man, you are going to end up in the penitentiary. The favor that you are about to get, you'll only get one time. I don't ever want to see you in court ever again. You got it?" "I promise," I replied. That was one promise I was sure to keep. And just as I promised, the lawyer or that judge never saw me again. That's been almost thirty years ago.

As for the guy, that I felt uneasy about from the beginning, I believe to this very day, he set us both up. Why do I believe that? Because he never called Mr. Ruthless to find out what was taking him so long or what happened to his merchandise. He laid a trap for me, but the Lord was on my side, even before I realized it was the Lord who was delivering me even back then.

BREAKING UP IS HARD TO DO

Even though I had just had a real close call, avoiding jail by the skin of my teeth, I failed to take all my lawyer's advice. I couldn't stay away from Mr. Ruthless. In my own strange way of coping, I remember I used to talk to my light-blue curtains that hung at my living room window. They reminded me of the big blue sky where hosts of heavenly angels and God dwells. I'd look at these curtains as if I was looking into heaven itself and I'd ask God was there something wrong with me? I didn't know that God was already working on me, calling me out of this loose lifestyle.

One particular time, Mr. Ruthless refused to come to my daughter's kindergarten graduation. He claimed that he didn't have time. I was livid. I told him, "You know what, you ain't never got to come to any of her graduations." At that time I didn't understand spiritual principles and the power that's in the spoken word. The Bible teaches that "death and life are in the power of the tongue..." (Proverbs 18:21). I spoke these words in the atmosphere, and they were fulfilled. He never made it to any of her graduations because he was locked up in the penitentiary.

I remember his seventh year in the penitentiary. He called me up and asked me if I would pray and ask God to release him out of jail. I said, "What makes you think that I can ask God to do that?"

He said, "Because I know you the one that prayed that I be in here."

I said, "Yeah, I did. But I also prayed and asked God not to kill you. I would prefer Him to lock you up than to let somebody kill you because I wanted my daughter to know her father."

Here's another time I tried to get away from Mr. Ruthless before he went to the penitentiary. One Sunday I was about to get in my car on my way to church, when he pulled up unannounced. He got out of his car and came over to me talking crazy. I thought "this ain't nothing but the devil." He's got his nerve! I haven't talked to you all day. I haven't talked to you all night. Now, here you come first thing on a Sunday morning, when I'm going to church, talking crazy. So I told him, "You know, you can go back where you came from."

He had just bought himself a drop-top BMW, trimmed in gold, with his nameplate all on the side. I didn't care what he was driving. He threw his car door open thinking that he could block me in. He was wrong! I backed out fast and took the door of that brand new gold BMW with me. That's right, I knocked his door clean off. Though I didn't make it to church, I received some satisfaction in that fact that he couldn't stop me. The only thing that I do regret about this incident is that my little cousin and my baby daughter were in the car with me. I know I scared my cousin to death. Unfortunately, she saw my ugly side. But as for my daughter, she was too young to remember this incident. Thank God.

I was finished with him. I told him that he was welcome to take all the stuff back. I just wanted out. I put everything on the table. I told him that he could have back the house, the jewelry, the furs, and the cars. But to my surprise, he refused to take anything back from me. He admitted that I deserved everything because of all the difficulty and danger I had put up with being with him. So I kept everything. For that I was grateful.

But it wasn't that easy. He came over to the house, and I didn't want to see him because every time I would see him, it looked like I would get weak for him. So if he came to the house, I wouldn't open the door. He kept beating on the door. My cousin was here from Atlanta. She jumped up out of bed wondering what was going on. Lo and behold, the brother kicked the door in. She ran out the back door. I ran out the back door. I asked her what she was running for. She told me because she was scared too. By that time, we called the police. Prior to the police arriving, I told her to go back in and see what was going on. She went back in the house. She later informed me that all he could say was, "I love this girl. I just don't like the way she talks to me. I love her, but she can't treat me any kind of way."

By the time the police got there, I found out that my name was not on the house. When he bought the house he had his lawyers place it in a land trust. I didn't know anything about the land trust, I always thought the house was legally mine. So, I could not even put him out of his own house. He had documents showing that. I was really humiliated over that situation.

Now don't get me wrong. We did have some good times in the years that we spent together. We would go on trips together, hang out or just whatever. Although, we had a lot of good times, our bad times outweighed those good times. The bigger he got in the drug game, the more strained our relationship would be because of all the different women, new friends coming out, and new enemies coming in. I was afraid for my life. I was afraid for my daughter's life. He had some Jamaicans that came on his team. I was afraid of them. You know, you see a bunch of Jamaicans, you don't know what's going to go down. I was afraid for my life all the time. Fear of the known and the unknown had become a way of life for me.

One day he asked me if he could meet me at home. When he got there, he had a suitcase—one of the biggest suitcases you could find. I asked him, "what was in the suitcase?" He opened it up like it was supposed to be a big surprise for me—it was full of cocaine. I wasn't surprised at all. I grabbed my daughter who was about nine or ten months old, and I went out on the front porch. He told me that somebody was going to come to my house and get this from me. I said, "No they won't. You will have to stay here or I will leave this in this house and nobody will get nothing." You better believe he stayed there because he knew when I said I wasn't going to do something; I wasn't going to do it. That's when I got in church and pleaded with God, and He truly delivered me out of this life. I never turned my back on God in that area any more.

Right before Mr. Ruthless left to go to the penitentiary, I found out that he got a young lady pregnant. One day while I was in the neighborhood, I popped up over his mother's house. This little baby was there. I asked her whose baby it was. She said it was her girlfriend's. Now at sixty-five years old, what kind of girlfriend does she have who has a little newborn baby? I asked her, "This is your girlfriend's baby? This ain't your grandbaby?"

She said, "No, this is my girlfriend's baby."

I called Mr. Ruthless up on the phone and said, "Your mother has a little baby at this house. Whose baby is it?"

He said, "I don't know whose baby that is."

However, I had already heard the word out on the street, so I told him, "I need you to meet me in front of my mother's house in twenty minutes." So you know he got all nervous and everything because he didn't know what I was going to say or do. Of course he met me at my mother's house. I got in the car with him and said, "Come on, let's drive off. Come on and take me out to dinner because we're going to have to talk about this. I need to hear this from you. I don't need to hear it from nobody else. I'm not going to fight you. I'm not going to argue with you. I'm not going to do anything. Is this your baby?" Then he said,

"I don't know why these women claim that I'm giving them a baby. I don't know what they're talking about."

I said, "Look, I know you. Those other people don't know you, but I do. Now I'm giving you a chance to come clean, to let me know if this baby is yours."

He looked at me and he said, "Yeah, I think so."

I got quiet. I said, "Okay." He dropped me back off at my momma's house. I got my little girl, we jumped in the car and drove all the way to Louisville, Kentucky, where one of my cousins lived. Thank God we made it there safely because I was mad and speeding. It took us about three-and-a-half hours to get there, when it normally takes about five hours. We weren't even there two days before my mother called. Mr. Ruthless had gone to my mother's house and told her that he had been robbed. He told her he needed to talk to me because I was the only one that could cool him down. Besides that, my house was the only place he could go to and be safe. In reality he could have gone to my house without me, he had the keys. But no, he needed me. My mother said, "He needs you. He really needs you and you need to call him." Evidentially, he was so pitiful that momma felt sorry for him.

So I called him, just to see what was up. Of course he

charmed me into coming back home. I came back to see about him, to make sure he wasn't hurt and to make sure everything was okay. I didn't come back to be his woman again. Once I returned he was able to get his thoughts together. He was going to terrorize the whole neighborhood until somebody told him about his stuff. He was ruthless like that. Finally, someone came forth. It was a young lady from the neighborhood. She was a dope fiend. All she needed was a little hit. She took him straight to the apartment where his identification, jewelry, and money was. What happened to the people who stole it, I don't know. But I'm sure it wasn't pleasant.

You may ask, how did this happen to Mr. Ruthless anyway? Well, of course he knew the person that robbed him. He was on the bus stop and Mr. Ruthless gave him a ride. He wore this big old five or six-carat ring on his baby finger. When they got ready to get out of his car, they snatched the ring off his finger and took off running.

After this whole ordeal, things really began to deteriorate for him. I couldn't trust him any more after that. I didn't believe anything he said after that. Even when he was telling the truth, I didn't believe him. But didn't let anybody bring me drama about him; I didn't let anybody come telling me he was doing this or doing that. I knew him. There wasn't anything that anyone could come tell me about him. I knew all about him. So if they called themselves pouring salt on him, they weren't getting any brownie points with me. There was a song out by Michele, called "Something in My Heart."

There was something in my heart that made him have a hook in me. Yes indeed, the brother had a hook in me. But then again, I wondered if it was really him or the money. The Bible says, "the love of money is the root of all evil." Not only did he love money, and he had a lot of it too.

While I was going through all of this, it may have appeared that my life was on hold, but it wasn't. I just didn't know when to move, so I had to wait on God, and when He came, it was right on time. All He was doing was getting me ready for my calling. He had to make sure that I was through with this life.

When I think about Mr. Ruthless, he really needed someone to build up his ego. People like his mother could see no wrong in him. She held him up as if he was the law. I remember her having a senior apartment. She let him use it as a hideaway. However, it wasn't, because he took women over there. And once you let a woman know, it's not a secret anymore. He called me one night and I asked him, "Are you at The Renaissance?" He said, "No." But I knew the background sounds because I had been there so many times. He thought once he talked to me, it was cool that night. It wasn't. I was the type of girl that you couldn't say just anything to. So I said, "Good night" with my mouth, but I was still troubled in my heart.

So I got up and went to the apartment. Since this was a senior citizen's building you had to be buzzed in to enter the apartment complex. Not wanting to alert him, I rang several bells except his mother's bell. Finally, someone that I didn't know answered the bell and asked, "Is that you?" Of course I answered, "Yes." But once I was in, I went straight up to Mr. Ruthless' mom's apartment. And to his surprise, there I was standing at his door. He did not know what to do. I asked, "Are you not gonna let me in?" But he wouldn't because he was hiding his girlfriend behind the door. I told her, "You better be scared."

So I went ahead and left. I wasn't going to do anything to her. I wasn't going to fight her. That's not what I did. I was too cute for all that. I didn't want to mess my face up. So I told him to have a good time, and I left. By the time I got home, here he comes. By playing it cool it put something on his mind. Now all of a sudden he wanted to know if I was okay. Yes, I was.

Every time this happened and Mr. Ruthless came to my house, I never knew if he was staying. I never wanted to ask because it would mess things up. I just went with the flow, but in my heart I knew the truth. That night, he stayed because he knew he was the one who was wrong. Evidently, he didn't care about the other sister. He wanted to see how I really felt. But it was too little, too late. I hung out with the bad boys, so I had to suffer many consequences—it was what it was.

LOOKING FOR MR. RIGHT

Being a hustler's woman was so much fun in the beginning. It was exciting living the high life. It was similar to being a celebrity because you had recognition, status and privileges. We wore the finest clothes, drove the nicest cars, had the expensive jewelry; diamonds, gold, and precious stones. And not to mention all the cash, there were times we had money coming out of our ears. But this type of life came with a very expensive price, and in the end, it was a price too high for me to pay. The truth was, from day-to-day you lived a lie, you believed that you were the hustler's favorite. And you believed it until you met or found out about all of the other favorites. Once they get you to where you're comfortable and you've gotten spoiled by all the ill-gotten gains, they change on you. Then they start to abuse you, and looking for fault in you, tearing your character down, belittling you, making you think you don't amount to anything. So I reached a breaking point where I was so weary with it all, that I just wanted out.

Therefore, I tried my best to run from this life, but it's like the devil was mad at me, and wasn't going to allow me to run away so fast. There were more tricks up his sleeve to destroy me once and for all. After Mr. Ruthless was sent away to prison, other hustlers were starting to pursue me. Oddly, one of the first ones who came after me was a hustler that looked identical to Mr. Ruthless. They could have been twins. My daughter would even be confused. Whenever she saw him, even she said, "Momma, he look like my daddy." When I heard that, I knew I had to run in the opposite direction. But this particular brother was trying to chase me, but thanks be to God he could never catch me. I am so glad that God stepped in and let me sidestep the trap that the devil set for me. About a month later, he was sitting in his van and somebody rode up on him and shot up his van killing him on the spot. The devil meant for me to be with him when that happened.

After him, another hustler came. He owned his own little cab stand. I was like, "God, what is this? I'm trying to run from these brothers. Where are they coming from?" Then another brother wanted to be with me who owned a lounge and everything. He was a nice person, but he wasn't good for me. I cried out, "Please, Lord, help me get away from them."

It was a test that I was going through. But I realized that I had to be the one to say no. God wasn't going to do that for me. I had to be the one who stood firm in what I wanted and what I believed in. At the time I didn't know a lot about the church, the Bible or God, but I did know that I didn't want another man who loved the streets, more than me.

I was looking for a man who could take me to God. That's who I thought I needed in my life. I knew there was more to life than just hustlers and the street life. I knew there was more depth to life than the sallow existence of chasing men and a fast buck. That's when I had an epiphany. In this one defining moment, I realized that no one could take me to God, but me. And that's when I had to fall to my knees, not just sometimes, but on a daily basis, to cry out for help. "Help me, Lord. I want to be your child. Help me be your servant. Help me to love myself." And God began to show me how to love myself as I got in the Word of God.

That's when I began to take another look at myself. I started loving me. I didn't have to go into rehab. I didn't have to go to a counseling or twelve-step program. All I had to do was be baptized in Jesus' name, filled with the precious gift of the Holy Ghost, and that's when my power started manifesting. I really thank God that I didn't lose my mind. God kept me safe all the way. The Lord kept moving and pushing me forward, and I didn't even know it. Though I was perplexed on every side, but Jesus was my solid rock. When I wanted to lash out, Jesus calmed the raging sea within my heart. Whenever I would fall, He would lift me up again. So I learned to cast all my cares on Him, because He proved that He really cared for me.

I thank God for the church, I really do. I never would have made it this far if it wasn't for the house of God and if it wasn't for the power of the Holy Ghost. Thank you, God, for letting me know that it is real. When I started turning things over to God, He began rearranging everything in my life. Yes, after I invited Jesus all the way into my life, everything changed for the better. I learned that you can't depend on anyone but God—and depend on God is exactly what I did. I decided to step out on faith and buy my own car. I went to the car dealer all excited. I think I took my cousin Junior with me to look at a Pontiac. It was brand new. Nobody had ever driven it. I was all excited and couldn't wait to talk to Mr. Ruthless so I could tell him that I got me a brand new car. When I called him and told him what I did, there was silence on the phone. A little puzzled, I asked him, "What's wrong? Aren't you excited about being able to buy my own car?"

He said, "Let me call you back."

I didn't hear from him for about three days. So I called his mother. I said, "What did I do to him? Is anything wrong with me buying my own car? I thought he would be happy for me." She said, "You don't know what's wrong with him?"

I said, "No, I don't."

She said, "He is jealous you went out and bought a car without him. You didn't need his money and now he feels like you don't need him anymore. Men like it when a woman has to depend on them. Your dependence is what empowers them. Obviously, you don't need him anymore. So that's why he's mad with you. But give him a few days. He'll be alright."

At that point I could really see. He always wanted to be the chief. He always wanted to run things. Nobody could do anything without him because he did have all the money. But he didn't understand that since I worked, I had my own source of income. After a while I got tired of depending on him for money. I just wanted to be able to do the things for myself that I wanted, with no strings attached.

Before he went to jail, Mr. Ruthless had left garbage bags and duffel bags of money with one of his sisters. He left babies behind. He didn't leave us any cash or anything. We didn't need it anyway because with God's help we were able to stand on our own. But his sister spent every dime of the money he left with her. By the time he got out the penitentiary, he had no money left. She didn't even offer us a loaf of bread, knowing that she was spending his money up. She never sent anything for his kids' birthdays. She never sent anything for Christmas, but she made sure she spent all their daddy's money, on herself.

When Mr. Ruthless went to jail, he was in a relationship with me and another young lady. But when he went to jail, he ended up marrying this young lady, which was good because it took the pressure off of me. I never stopped my daughter from going to see her father. When she got about the age of nine years old, she said, "Momma, I don't want to go see my daddy again in prison. I'm not the one that did wrong, so why do the police officers have to search me, and I haven't done anything wrong?" I never stopped her from going, but once she was old enough, I let her make that decision.

I am so grateful to God. My daughter could have been without a father or mother in her life, because I could have gone to jail along with Mr. Ruthless. And, my other family members that I recruited in the drug business could have gone to jail too on account of me. I was so blind and dumb. Everything I did with this man placed my life in peril. But thank God for Jesus. He always covered us, even though we didn't deserve His mercy and grace, yet He still showed mercy on us.

Chapter 6

THE WORKER

Deliver me, O my God, out of the hand of the wicked, out of
the hand of the unrighteous and cruel man. For thou art my
hope, O LORD GOD: thou art my trust from my youth.
Psalm 71:4-5

As I continued on my journey, I met the acquaintance
of this young man in whom I will refer to as Mr. Worker, for
the simple fact that he actually had a respectable, everyday
nine-to-five job. This was a first for me. I never had a man
that worked a regular job before. In the beginning this was
quite an adjustment for me because I wasn't used to waiting
on a paycheck to come or clear. Even though I was not depending upon him for financial support, I had to wait on
him to take me out.

He was a nice guy, but he was not a go getter. He did not
have any dreams or aspirations outside of going to work for
someone else every day. Whether by nature or necessity he
was on the frugal side. But he didn't mind feasting off other
people, he was quick to accommodate others generosity.

Despite these little differences we enjoyed each other. Mr. Worker enjoyed dancing. He was a great stepper. That was right up my alley because I loved to step too. We would attend a lot of stepper's sets and win all kinds of stepping dance contests. People would come up to us and put fifty dollars in our hands because we danced so well together. Everyone thought that we made a good couple, so the time came for me to introduce Mr. Worker to my family.

I knew that Mr. Worker was quite different from the previous men in my life, but when I introduced him to my family, they laughed when they saw him. He dressed a different way than the players, the pimps and the hustlers. He was a totally different man. He was a shirt and slacks man, a shirt and tie man, where the others had alligators, crocodiles, eel skins, and silk suits. He didn't have an up-to-date car. They were use to me jumping out of Rolls Royces, Corvettes, Mercedes Benzes, Cadillacs and BMWs. Every car Mr. Ruthless had was top of the line and I was able to drive any car that he had, plus I had my own nice rides too. But Mr. Worker didn't have any of that. I don't believe he ever owned a new car, let alone and expensive one.

One good thing about Mr. Worker was that he went to church every now and then. However, that wasn't good enough for me because I wanted somebody to push me closer to my Lord and Savior, even though we were still living in sin. Nevertheless, I know God sent him into my life to teach me about small things that I took for granted. I didn't know how to be grateful for small things because I was so accustomed to getting the biggest and the best things. He taught me how to be grateful for that. He taught me how to be grateful for getting a twenty-dollar bill. When Mr. Worker would give me twenty dollars, I would look at him like, "Oh, my God, what's this?" I was accustomed to getting big money. If I asked for two or three hundred dollars, or five hundred dollars from the hustlers, I would get that. But God had to break me from that by teaching me to respect what people gave, particularly when it's from their heart.

A Word from the Lord: "You're Going to be a First Lady"

I tried to be involved with Mr. Worker for as long as I could. I wanted it to work because I knew the change was good for me. It was my way of searching for and living a better life, but the Lord had different plans for me. The more I was with him, the more I would also hear the Lord's voice speaking to me. On one occasion he and I had a discussion about taking our relationship to the next level. After spending the night together, I was lying awake when all of a sudden the Lord spoke to me. It was just as loud and clear as if somebody else was in the room.

He said, "Carrie, you cannot continue doing this because I have called you to be a first lady."

With a puzzled look on my face, I turned and looked over at Mr. Worker and asked him,

"Are you going to be a pastor?"

"Oh yeah, you know people say I sound just like one," he responded.

However, when he said that, I knew then, he was not the one who the Lord had chosen. I got up out of my bed. I went into the living room. It was a bright sunshiny beautiful day. I looked up toward heaven and I asked God if this was Him really talking to me, I needed to know. The Lord said, "Pick up the Bible." I picked up the Bible and began to read in the book of Matthew. When I began to read, God began to start speaking to me. He let me know that my lifestyle was not right, and not pleasing to Him. As I kept reading the Word, I could feel my soul being revived. I couldn't put the Bible down.

Every day I would run home to get the Bible because I wanted to read more of God's Word. As I continued reading the Word, I was being cleansed, inside and out. Even though I now started to realize the importance of having a relationship with the Lord, I was still going to skating parties and having cocktails at night when we went out. I still had not fully committed my way unto the Lord. I remained a seeker for eight years until God fully cleaned me up.

I would tell my sisters and my friends, "The Lord told me I was going to be a pastor's wife," and they would laugh at me because they knew the lifestyle that I came from and was still living. And knowing all that, me becoming a pastor's wife was completely hilarious to one of my sisters. She used to go around and fake like she was speaking in tongues, mocking me. I just let her mock me. I started going to church, every time the doors of the church were open. I would be there asking God for His help. However, the more I went to church, the more Mr. Worker started disliking me.

By this time, I had allowed him to move into my house. But once I did that, it was hard to get him out. I told him, "You have to go." He didn't want to go, because he was the type who would freeload if you let him. Besides, he had the better end of the deal being with me. I had my own house, my own money, everything. So I put my foot down and I told him, "You can't stay here anymore. You need to go."

However, the Lord told me, "Don't just put him out. Give him an ultimatum." So I gave Mr. Worker an ultimatum; either leave in peace or get put out. God also told me to not to be angry or vengeful, but to mean what I say. When April of that year came, I put up a petition before the Lord that Mr. Worker would leave in peace. I didn't want any arguments, fussing or fighting. And the Lord had me to give him a specific move out date. But by this time he was really beginning to get on my nerves so I was trying to get him to leave before the move out date. However, he didn't want to leave.

One day I was so fed up with him that I became angry and pulled out my pistol and was like, "Look, just get out of my house." I had gotten sick of looking at him. But even with me and Smith & Western starring him in the face, he still wouldn't move. If anyone should have been praising God at that moment for my deliverance it was him!

Suddenly, my son came out the room and grabbed the gun from me, because the devil had gotten me mad enough to shoot him. My son looked at Mr. Worker and shouted, "didn't my momma say she don't want you in this house? Don't you know when a woman don't want you no more?"

Mr. Worker still refused to go. That's when my son cocked the pistol to shoot him. At that very second, I saw death in my house. So I began to plead with my son, "No, don't shoot him, he's not worth throwing your life away or getting the electric chair." I knew at that moment the devil had set another trap to change the course of my life. He was trying to prevent me from fulfilling the prophesy, that God had given me about becoming a preachers wife. This incident was so traumatic for my son that I sent him away to Mississippi for the summer. Apparently, the stress of life was taking a toll on him too, and this incident almost pushed him over the edge. It was good for him to get away from Chicago.

The final days that Mr. Worker was in my house were some difficult days. However, one day I came home from work and found his clothes were gone, his shoes were gone, he was gone and he left the keys on the table. I ran through my house happy and excited, praising God. The Lord had lifted an eight hundred pound gorilla off of my back. In Matthew 11:28-30, the Lord says the He will give you His rest; He will take your heavy burdens and give you His light burden. Yes indeed, I was as light as a feather and free as a bird. I was so happy, but I didn't call down to Mississippi to tell my son the good news about Mr. Worker moving out.

However, after being down there for a while, my son called me and he told me, "Momma, I'm ready to come home. All they do around here is gossip and I'm bored to death." He said, "Momma, you know that you don't like all that gossiping so, if you don't want me to become a gossiper, you better send for me to come home." He was manipulating me, but it was fine I didn't mind him coming back home. So I sent for him and told him to call me when he arrived back in town.

About a week later, he called me to let me know, he'd made it home. I asked him, "Where are you at?"

"I'm in the house," he replied.

"In the house? How did you get in the house" I replied with great concern.

He said, "Mr. Worker let me in."

"Okaaay," I calmly responded. I didn't want to put my son in a position where there would be a confrontation between himself and Mr. Worker. I didn't let my son know that Mr. Worker was not supposed to be in my house. I had forgotten to tell my son about Mr. Worker finally moving out. As soon as I got off work, I called a locksmith and had him change all the locks. Three days went by. Mr. Worker called me back and said, "Oh, I see you finally changed the locks." What unmitigated gall! This man had been coming back to my house lying up like he was still living there. Then I remembered, that one day when I came home I had the feeling that someone had been in there, because certain things were out of position and it struck me as being odd, but I shrugged it off. After that incident, he didn't attempt to reenter my house again.

With him out of direct contact with me (because he still lurked around), I began to focus more on my children, the Lord, and on living a saved and sanctified life.

Even though I had moved on, Mr. Worker had not and he too, started stalking me. He was outside of my job every day. It wasn't like Mr. Skater hiding in the bushes, no Mr. Worker was in plain sight. He would conspicuously sit across the street and watch my clients go in and out my shop. Weeks and months went by, and this man just kept rolling by. But all he could see is that it was just me and Jesus. He even came to the church a few times. I would turn around and look up, and there he would be sitting up in the balcony. I was like, "Lord Jesus, what in the world is this brother's problem?" But I couldn't stop him from going to public places.

It was during times like these that I began to fall in love with Jesus. He was the only man that I could trust. I fell so in love with God that I didn't want to share my time with anybody. When I would leave work, I would come home and it would be me and the Lord. My car radio stayed on the gospel stations. I turned my business into a Christian atmosphere. I lost some clients because some of them said they couldn't take the religious music, but I gained some new ones. To those who were now seeing the new Carrie, they thought I had changed overnight. They didn't realize that God had been working on me for years, and that it had been a long arduous road to my deliverance. It took all of these experiences for me to allow His light to shine through me, because I was covered in darkness for a long time.

I remember my bishop once said that some of you were baptized when you were little children because your parents told you, but some of you need to get baptized again because you want to. I contemplated about that and I got baptized again because I did it for me this time. I was so excited when I got baptized again. Being saved now, I began to attract different types of men. But men, like the drug dealers who were still in darkness, they didn't like me anymore. Everything about me had changed. My appearance and my countenance had changed. My clothing had changed. My hair had changed. I even put on a few extra pounds. So now when those hustlers saw me, they would run the other way, because I was walking in the light. How happy I was to see that. In St. John 3:19 the Bible says that, "men loved darkness rather than the light because their deeds were evil." Since I was no longer in darkness, so the hustlers "comprehended it not."

THE REAL HUSTLER
MY FATHER

*I*n chapter six of the book of Ephesians, there are a couple passages of scriptures that are dear to my heart. They read as follows:

> Honour thy father and mother; (which is the first commandment with promise;) That it may be well with thee, and thou mayest live long on the earth. And, ye fathers, provoke not your children to wrath: but bring them up in the nurture and admonition of the Lord.
>
> Ephesians 6:2-4

I truly believe that this is one of the most important passages of scripture in the Bible. Why, because it deals with family dynamics and relationships. The first word in the passage is honor. To honor means to hold in high respect, to give special merit and to hold in esteem. That's how it is supposed to be when a child looks at their parents—honor. Parents should be a child's role model, not an athlete or some entertainer. They should be their child's mentor, where they learn love and respect, responsibility and morals, how to be productive individuals, how to love and appreciate God, and also how to love themselves in order to love others. This should all come from a relationship with their father and mother.

On the other hand, this same passage warns fathers not to make their children angry. When children are not given the love support and admonition from their loving parents, here is where children can go astray. Parents can be too over bearing, too unreasonable, too sheltering, too easy going, without giving the consequences necessary for a child to learn from their mistakes. This was the problem in each one of the men that I talk about in this book. Either they received too much and became spoiled or too little love and nurturing, and became monsters.

As for me, though I was raised by a very supportive mother and a wonderful stepfather, the die had already been cast. The first six years of my life were already marked by living with an unstable and violent man—my father. At a young age, our family had to adapt to the chaotic environment that he created. Unfortunately, that left a lasting impression. This is why we see what Ephesians says, fathers provoke not your children to anger. In other words, fathers don't force situations on your children that cause them to become bitter. A bitter heart affects how a child sees the world around them, and it also affects how they will interact with the people around them. With good role models, a child has a very good chance of being a well-rounded individual; the opposite is true with bad role modeling.

In Proverbs 22:6, the Bible teaches, "Train up a child in the way he should go: and when he is old, he will not depart from it." We all know this is true. But what if a child is trained up in the wrong thing—they won't depart from that either. This is why dysfunctional cycles are so hard to break, particularly if they have been planted at an early age. Often times, parents do not realize that they are training a child. But the fact is we are training a child whenever they are observing us. Children pick up everything that their parents do; the good, the bad, and the ugly.

The last hustler in my life, turned out to actually be the real hustler in my life—my father. My daddy and I reunited when I was twenty-six years old. It had been twenty years since we had any real contact with each other. My brother had gotten shot and somehow my father found out about it. How he got here and from where he came, I am not certain. But according to him, he came to help my brother get back on his feet. In the midst of this tragic event, dad's coming was particularly good news. We were excited about our father coming to Chicago, particularly since we hadn't seen him since we were all young children. Now all of a sudden, here he is. We hadn't had any dealings with him in all these years, so it was exciting and a bit awkward at the same time. Many things had changed in our lives. We weren't the same little children that he had known. We were all grown up now, living our own lives. There were grandchildren in whom he had only heard about, but never met. And all the grandkids were excited about meeting their "real grandfather," as they would say. Even though my stepfather was the one in their lives, there remained a longing in their lives to meet their real grandfather. The same longing that I had. He was as much a mystery to me as he was to them.

When he came, they were ecstatic about him because he was so full of joy and life. He was fun loving and played with them all the time. He would do fun things with them like take them to the park, or taking them to get ice cream. He wasn't mean to them at all. He was playful like a lovable teddy bear. And you know how kids love to be around people who are fun and can make them laugh. This was very refreshing for me to witness, because I never knew my father had a fun side to him. Oh, how I wished that I would have had the opportunity to play with my father. But that was a part of himself that he never gave to us.

My dad stayed with my brother until he recuperated from his gunshot wound. However, my brother discovered that my dad was stealing his money and other small items. My brother didn't want a thief living with him even if it was our father. So my dad had to move from my brother's place to one of my sisters for a little while. Thank God, he never stole anything from her. Then after he stayed with my sister, he moved in with me.

While dad was with me, the longer he stayed, the more his old self began to surface. One of the first disappointing things that I found out about him was that he was an alcoholic. He didn't just drink, but he would drink to the point of passing out. Soon he was known as a drunk to the people in the community. It was embarrassing because everyone knew he was my father. People would call me at work and tell me, "Carrie, come get your daddy. He's out on the street sloppy drunk." Though it broke my heart to see him in that condition, I still honored my father and I would go get him as soon as I got off work.

The funny thing about my father was, with all of his weaknesses and bad habits, when sober he was a likable person. He met women who took a liking to him, but not enough for them to let him live with them. So I continued being the one who was responsible for him and would still have to go drag my daddy home from the streets.

Growing up I use to always hear people say, "no matter who you are, you are good at something." That was certainly true of my father. Daddy was an awesome cook. He could have had a great career as a chef. He was also very good cleaning house—a little too good. One particular time, I had my mortgage money hidden in the pockets of an old leather skirt in the back of the closet. I hardly ever wore it, so I felt it was a good place to keep some money. When I came home from work one day, my house was all cleaned up. But there was something that was very unusual. Every door in my house was closed; the bedrooms the bathrooms, every room.

Dad had cooked me a big dinner. All the pots were still on the stove. He had thrown down. He'd prepared a duck, sweet potatoes, collard greens, and cornbread. I had a bottle of champagne that was given to me years ago for my birthday. I never touched it but kept it around for decoration. Now, it was gone. Immediately, I had a bad feeling. Something was wrong with this picture. Right then I started praying "Lord, please don't let me find this man in one of these rooms dead. I opened up all the doors slowly. Every time I opened up one of those doors, all I found was an immaculately cleaned room.

Four days went by and still no sign of dad. By this point, I wasn't sure if I should call in a missing persons report or not. But the next day when my mortgage payment was due, I went to my closet where my money was stashed and discovered that the mortgage money was gone. I was devastated that my own father had ripped me off.

A few days after I discovered that my money was gone, he came back like nothing ever happened. But instead of being mad, I couldn't find it in me to be upset with him. In place of anger I had pity. Besides, my anger wouldn't have changed him in the slightest way, because he was already a tortured soul. He was a man left to his own devises and on the road to self-destruction—a man with good potential that was never realized. So who was I to judge him? Setting aside my anger and disappointment, I forgave him and I continued to let him stay in my house.

My brother happened to give me a bunch of money, several thousands of dollars, to hold for him. I put it in one of my thigh-high boots, calling myself hiding it again in the back of the closet. And with the fantastical thinking of a little girl who didn't want to see no wrong in her father, I believed that daddy wouldn't steal from me again. I was wrong. He stole a couple thousand of that money. That was the last straw.

Heartbroken and devastated, I called my mother and stepfather in tears. After everything that I tried to do for him, I just couldn't understand how he would do this to me. But now, I had reached a breaking point. I told my mother, "I didn't care what condition he was in, whether he was on the street corner drunk or sleeping on a park bench, he would never be stepping foot back in my house again. He'd never get the chance to steal another dime from me and my children." Patiently, my mother listened, as I ranted, she never said a word. My stepfather told me, "do what you have to do, and don't feel bad about it. So I did just that—I cut ties with my daddy.

Looking back at it, these were not the first times that daddy had ever taken something from me. He had been stealing from me all of my life, ever since I was a little girl. So, I was surprised, but then, not surprised. Daddy had stolen the loving father image that I needed so badly. He had taken away the security that I needed to feel safe. He took away all the important moments of my life where he should have been there. He stole away his counsel and wisdom about life that he should have been there to teach me. All he left was the memories of a no good man. That is why as a young girl I was filled with bitterness and rebellion and I ended up seeking those same traits in other bad men. As a rebellious young woman, I became trapped in daddy's cycle of dysfunction that took me years to escape.

Being the charmer that he was, he ended up finding a lady friend named Rose. She let my daddy move in with her. She did everything she could to help my daddy out. She was a nice lady. But when he started drinking, she would call me up to see what I could do to help him. But you can't do anything with somebody who is sloppy drunk. It's like talking to a brick wall. You simply cannot help someone who doesn't want help. Being inebriated was the state that my daddy preferred to be in. There is nothing that someone else could do about that.

One particular December, my sisters and I decided to go and celebrate my mother's birthday down in Mississippi. Some time ago she had purchased a summer home down there, where she would go when it is winter in Chicago. Somehow, my dad found out that we were going down there and now he wanted to go too. He pleaded, "Please let me go with you, just drop me off down there in Mississippi because that's where I'm going to die."

When he said that, I didn't believe him, because it wasn't the first time that he'd ever said that. My response was, "Every year you tell me you're going to die." But in the long run, we allowed him to go with us. As he got in the car, he passed me twenty dollars. I snatched that twenty dollars so fast. They were like, "Why did you snatch the money like that?" I replied, "Girl, he might change his mind. This is the first time he ever gave me something. So you know I'm going to take this, and he ain't getting it back." So we all laughed at my humorous response that just so happened to be a good note to begin a long drive to Mississippi.

As he requested we dropped him off once we were a good way into Mississippi. Not too long after that, one of my aunties called me and let me know that he had sunken down to his lowest state. So once again, I felt sorry for him, and felt a sense of responsibility to go see him. They had put him in a nursing home.

When I walked into the nursing home day-room I saw him sitting in his wheelchair. There were several other residents sitting in there as well. Some watching television, others starring out the window. When I saw him I was shocked and deeply saddened. He was sitting there in his wheel chair looking out of the window. Daddy had lost all his weight and was down to about eighty pounds. He had forth stage lung cancer and was so sick that he could barely talk. He turned around and saw my face, and he did a double take. He was surprised to see his baby girl. He wheeled himself over to me. When he got over to me, I gave him a big o' hug. Then he took me to his room. He went over to his dresser and started pulling his clothes out the drawers. He obviously thought I was there to take him home. It was so sad. I put my hand on his shoulder and I said, "Daddy, I'm sorry, but I'm not here to take you home. I can't take you with me because there is no one in my house to take care of you."

Immediately, that upset him. He got in his bed and turned his face to the wall. I felt so bad. Daddy felt so dejected. I tried to comfort him but, he stayed turned away from me. Before I left the room, I said, "See you daddy. I love you." He didn't wave goodbye. He remained motionless. I walked over to him and kissed him goodbye and then left the nursing home. Once I got into my car and called my brothers and sisters. I told them if they wanted to see him for the last time, they'd better hurry up and get down there, because he didn't have much longer to live. And just as daddy prophesied, the following June, he passed away there in Mississippi.

Before he died, I got a chance to talk to him one last time. I asked him; why out of all the children he stole the most from me. His answer was surprising. He told me that I was the only one who would keep forgiving him. When I was a little girl, I used to write letters to him and put them in an envelope. That's as far as they ever got, because my momma didn't know where she was to mail them. In my mind, I knew that if I could get this letter to him, he would eventually call me or come see me.

I used to write in the letter, "Daddy, am I pretty enough for you? Daddy, do you love me? What did I do to you to cause you not to come see me?" At this time, I didn't know my father was in prison. All I remembered everyone saying that he was in Macon, Georgia. So that made me want to go to Macon, Georgia. I was always hoping somebody would take me to Macon, Georgia. When people used to say they were going out of town, I used to say, "Where you going?" When they would say where, I would be like, "Oh, I'm trying to get to Macon, Georgia."

That same little girl lived inside me all these years. In a sense I've been going to Macon Georgia to see my daddy all of my life. I didn't realize it wasn't my fault that daddy wasn't there. I was just a little girl, how could I have ever known. So I grew up with a big hole in my heart longing to be validated by my father—an innocent little girl's first love is supposed to be her daddy. That's who I was looking for all these years. So to fill the void that daddy had left inside me, I became attracted to the hustlers. All of them, Mr. Ice, Mr. Skater, Mr. Worker, and Mr. Ruthless, just stops along the way on my journey to "Macon, Georgia."

So in the end, I received my little girl's wish. I wanted to see him and God gave me a chance to see him. I enjoyed it while it lasted. Even though he used me and stole from me, God gave me that chance to see my father.

My father was the oldest of nine, but he was the only one who turned out bad. The question is why did he turn out the way he did? The answer is, my grandmother really spoiled him. That's what messed him up. Mothers must be careful how they raise their boys because they make them turn out thinking that the world owes them something. And one of the ways this false sense of entitlement manifests itself, is the ill-treatment of women. One of the worst things you can do to a child is to give them everything. Sometimes parents make the mistake of trying to buy their children's affection. Not only does this not work, but the children build up resentment towards the parents that do this. All the child really wants from the parents is them, not things.

From what I hear, all my dad's brothers used to work, but not my dad. He wasn't interested in earning a living the honest way. Apparently, he thought that he could get by on his looks because he was a real handsome type. He was about five-two and a little bow legged like my brother. Though he was blessed with good looks, he was also cursed with no good ways. He was having affairs with married women. While unsuspecting husbands were leaving out of the front door going to work, daddy was sneaking in the back door to commit adultery.

So, clearly my father was a man who lacked any morals. But he did have some good brothers and sisters. They used to help take care of us. We had an Uncle Junior that no matter where we were, my Uncle Junior would come visit us. My Uncle Andrew would come see us. We would go down to my grandmother's house in the summer time and spend the summer with my other aunties and uncles. Some of them were just a couple years older than us because my grandmother had two sets of children. She had four adult children, and then later on she had five more.

I realize that my dad came back and lived off of me. He never took care of me, and never did anything for me but give me that twenty dollar bill. Thank God my mother didn't raise us to become bitter at him because he wasn't around. Growing up, my mother never talked negative about our father. So by her not saying anything bad about him that left open the door for us to still want to see him and love him all the more. In this, she was very wise because she didn't want to poison our minds against our father. Therefore, she never talked about our father in a disparaging way. She let us make our own decisions about our father.

My Salvation
Experience

Who hath saved us, and called us with an holy calling, not according to our works, but according to his own purpose and grace, which was given us in Christ Jesus before the world began.
2 Timothy 1:9

After all I had gone through with the different men in my life, there was something that they all had in common; none of them was able to bring fulfillment into my life. Though it is true that there were some important things that I missed out on when I was a little girl, the fact is my dad could have never fulfilled me. Though I sought fulfillment by entering into many unhealthy and unholy relationships with other men, none of them was able to fulfill me. Though I wore the finest of clothes, drove expensive imported cars, ate at the finest restaurants, and had plenty of money, none of those material things could fulfill me, and neither could they make me happy.

In the book of Ecclesiastes, Solomon makes this observation:

117

...I had great possessions of great and small cat-
tle above all that were in Jerusalem before me: I
gathered me also silver and gold, and the pecu-
liar treasure of kings and of the provinces: ...So I
was great, and increased more than all that were
before me in Jerusalem: ...And whatsoever mine
eyes desired I kept not from them, I withheld not
my heart from any joy; for my heart rejoiced in all
my labour: Then I looked on all the works that
my hands had wrought, and on the labour that I
had laboured to do: and, behold, all was vanity
and vexation of spirit, and there was no profit under the sun.

Ecclesiastes 2:7-11

King Solomon, the wisest king that ever lived, was a man
who had it all. He had power, fame, wealth, and women. He
held back no pleasure from himself. Solomon was a man
that, "did it to the max." But after indulging every enticement
and engaging all of his passions for lust, he walked away with
this ageless truth, "...all was vanity and vexation of spirit, and
there was no profit under the sun."

I walked a similar road. I tried men, money, and merchandise but in the end, it only made me miserable. So
after spending years of going around in circles during my
wilderness experience, I came face-to-face with this simple
but tremendous question that Jesus asks in Mark 8:36, "...
what shall it profit a man, if he shall gain the whole world,
and lose his own soul?" In Revelation 3:8 Jesus: rebuked
the Laodicean Church for their dependence upon material

wealth. He admonished them saying, "I counsel thee to buy of me gold tried in the fire, that thou mayest be rich…" Then in verse 20, He makes his final appeal to the Laodiceans, the same one He made to me, "Behold, I stand at the door, and knock: if any man hear my voice, and open the door, I will come in to him, and will sup with him, and he with me." It wasn't until I opened the door of my heart to the right man that I finally found fulfillment—that man is Jesus.

This was a transitional time in my life. I was attending a Baptist church at the time, however, my spirit man wasn't being fed. There was still an emptiness within me even during and after I left the services. I didn't quite understand that God was calling me away from that church to another. All I knew was there was somewhere else I was supposed to be. One day, my brother invited me to come hear this Bishop preach at his church on the Southside of Chicago. But it wasn't just an invitation; my brother insisted that I come hear this man of God. I took my brother up on his initiation and came to the Apostolic Pentecostal Church of Morgan Park, under the leadership of Bishop William A. and First Lady Mary P. Ellis (2012).

When I arrived at the church that Sunday morning, the church was packed with thousands of people. The spirit was high in the church. There was a great atmosphere of praise and worship. You could feel the Spirit moving through the congregation. My soul was revived as I drank the living water that flowed from the outpouring of the Holy Spirit. Then came time for the message, Bishop Ellis stood behind the pulpit and preached the house down. Though the church was packed with thousands of people, it was as if Bishop was preaching directly to me. I really felt the power of God. The service impacted me so much that I came back for Bible class the following Wednesday. I returned on Friday night but this time I brought my cousin with me who had flown in from Atlanta. We were both enjoying the service and I told her then, this is the church that I'm going to join. As soon as I said that, Bishop Ellis said, "if you think you just gon' slip up in this church without me talking to your pastor first, you got another thing coming." I was amazed. It was if the man of God and I were already connected. When the following Wednesday came, I spoke with Bishop Ellis after the service and I told him that I wanted to join the church. I also explained that I was baptized at twelve years old, but now I wanted to be baptized in the name of Jesus, at the age of thirty-three, but this time I was doing it for myself.

After I was baptized in Jesus' name, I tarried for the Holy Ghost and the Lord lit me up. When the Holy Ghost fell upon me, I began to speak in tongues as the Holy Ghost gave utterance. It was glorious. It was marvelous. I had never felt anything like the Holy Spirit before in my entire life. I remember how I use to laugh at people dancing in the spirit, shouting and speaking in tongues, now I knew what all the excitement was about—being saved, delivered and set free. Hallelujah! I knew a change had come on me when I received the power of the Holy Ghost. I needed that power. I needed the comforter. I needed a relationship with my heavenly Father, because He was the only one that could fill the gaping hole in my soul.

Now I had a new walk, and a new talk, but the journey and the battle had just begun. I had some serious soul searching to do. Like the Gospel song says, "won't He make you clean inside" so I asked God to show me my real self, and He did. Like going into surgery, the Lord opened me up so He could operate. He showed me what was on the inside of me, and I didn't like what I saw. It was as though I was looking into the window of my heart and I saw all that filthy sin. Thank God I was close to my bed because I collapsed on my bed after seeing how ugly I was. I began to cry just like the woman with the alabaster box. Being in deep contrition, I asked Him to clean me up and make me over again. I wanted to be beautified with salvation. That was the beginning of an eight year process to get me ready for the person and place that God called me to be. It wasn't easy, I had to fight every step of the way. But thanks be to God that gives us the victory and causes us to triumph over the enemy.

I still was attractive and I still liked men. God didn't take away my natural desires for a man, but He taught me how to keep those desires under control. Men were still coming my way. But as soon as they opened up their mouth, I knew whether it would turn out to be a waste of my time. God taught me how to be wise. So, I began to question every man who tried to approach me. I asked them point blank, were they saved and did they know Jesus? They would usually fumble around trying to find an answer and respond saying,

"Well, you know, I heard about Him." Immediately I knew to strike that one. Then another would come along and say, "Well, I'll follow you to church." Nope, not him either. He needs to be following Jesus on his own, not following me. So I just had to keep on moving on and keep trusting God to show me the right one.

During this time, there were so many sisters getting married. That made me want to be married even more. But it wasn't time for me to be married; it was time for me to be closer to Christ. In a sense, I only had time to be God's bride. He wanted me for Himself, so He could teach me how to be a holy bride. This is something that no man could have ever taught me. So I learned how to keep myself in celibacy.

It was a blessing being celibate. It was a blessing not having to answer to anyone other than Jesus. I didn't have to get dressed up and put on makeup all the time. I didn't have to do anything I didn't want to do. It was exciting. I could serve the Lord as much as I wanted to, or stay in church as long as I wanted to. I could do as many godly things as I saw fit. It was truly a blessing. I didn't have to argue with or fuss at anyone. All I had to do was just love on God.

I would have my Bible in my bed with me, waking up with it, going to bed with it. It was like the best sleep I ever had. When the enemy would bring doubt and fear to my mind or try to tempt me, I would play gospel music. I learned there is power in praise and worship music because it wars against the enemy and demonic spirits with chains. Playing gospel music at night sets such a peaceful atmosphere. There's nothing like the rest you get when praise music plays throughout the night.

It was truly a blessing waiting on the Lord. However, there were nights that I cried because I was lonely and longed for the companionship of a loving man. I often wondered what was taking God so long to bring my Mr. Right, into my life. But I would quickly snap out of it, because deep inside I knew the Lord was still working on me, and the time had not yet come.

One of the most difficult aspects of waiting on the Lord to provide your mate, is fending off those would be stumbling blocks. About three or four guys would call me and attempt to date me. But I wasn't about to interrupt the relationship that I was having with the Lord. And then there was the pressure that I received from my sisters, who use to tease me saying, "I had cobwebs all over me because I hadn't been with a man in years." But they didn't know the peace, the joy and the happiness that I had by being obedient to the Lord and waiting on Him.

As time went by, the devil tried tempting me to satisfy my needs through the flesh. He would taunt me saying that I was getting too old; and that I should hurry up to get married. He then said that my biological clock was ticking; and if I wanted more kids I needed to hurry up. At first I resisted, but soon I began to give in. The Spirit was willing but my flesh was weak. Therefore, I allowed the enemy to coax me out of my ark of safety. And I gave in and was intimate with a man.

That was the most hurtful and heartfelt thing that I had ever felt. I cried like a baby. I was so heartbroken over my weakness and learned to never have confidence in the flesh. I let someone come between me and the Lord. It was the first time that I ever really fell in love—it was with Jesus. When we are tempted to sin, God always provides a way of escape. He told me to back away and leave him alone. God told me that he wasn't the one. But I kept telling God, "Yes he is." Then He sent a little girl, which is my cousin, to let me know that this man wasn't the one. He sent a sister that I hadn't seen in years to let me know that he wasn't the one. My first lady and my pastor told me he wasn't the one. And I disobeyed everybody. Then He warned me saying, "Don't do it. If you do it, I'm going to turn the fire up under you." Still, I was disobedient and did it anyway.

Sure enough, God turned the fire of conviction up so high on me that I could begin to feel my flesh burning. He wanted me to feel this fire. I had many restless nights, being tormented not from demons but God convicting me. God's conviction is worse than anything the devil can do. If the devil is on your tail, you can call on God to help you. But if God is on your tail, there is nothing or no one that can help you. When God is your problem, then only God is your answer.

The price was high for disobeying God. God knew that I was going to be able to weather the storm. He knew that I wasn't going to quit because He chastised me. I often heard my pastor say, God chastens who He loves. Like so many of the men that I dealt with in the past, God was not abusive;

124

His loving chastening brought healing and made me a better person. He knew that I wasn't going to just throw in the towel, but I was going to fight this thing to the end.

I didn't go seeking other people's advice, asking what I should do. I didn't go running and crying to my mother and father, besides, what could they do? All I did was take my heavy burdens to the Lord, and He heard my cry. I became much more sensitive to His voice. When God said go, I knew that was Him. And when God was finished with me, I never looked back. I wasn't willing to test the Lord again, and meet with tragic consequences as Lot's wife did. No, I was careful not to disobey the Lord again.

Yes, the devil tried to come and shame me because I slipped and fell. But, I kept my head up high. I didn't walk around with my head down because I made mistakes. I fell down many times, but I kept getting back up. I got knocked down a couple of times but I got back up. I never quit. I still knew how to come back and repent on a daily basis. I know how to reverence the Lord. I know that no one is in control but God. I didn't have any control over my own life, because I was no longer my own, but I had been bought with a price. What the devil meant for my destruction, God meant for my good. All the devil actually did was caused me to get closer to God.

Therefore, I count it as a good thing because all that slip did is let me know that I had not arrived yet and that the Lord wasn't through with me yet. He taught me that love covers a multitude of sins. That's where the real power is—love. God is love. It's a blessing that you can love your enemies.

It's a blessing when you can go back to the ones who mistreated you and tell them thank you, because if it wasn't for what they did, I wouldn't be who I am today. Yes, you meant it for evil, but God meant it for good. It's a blessing that they know you forgive them, whether you did wrong or they did wrong to you. It's just an exciting feeling when you can go to somebody and say, "I appreciate you. You forced me into the arms of a man who shed his blood and died for me. I appreciate you because you caused me to seek out a man that I never knew. But today, I know him, and his name is Jesus." It's such a blessing being saved.

As I began to wait on God to give me a husband, I began to work in the ministry. I was faithful in the ministry. I paid my tithes and my offerings. Every time the doors of the church were open, I was available. I never missed Sunday school. I didn't miss prayer meeting. I worked on the hospitality committee until they made me president. I took it as just not standing at the door greeting people, but I looked at it as a ministry. I would pray for the people as they came in and out the doors of the sanctuary. They didn't even know that I was interceding for them, but I was. God had given me the spirit of discernment and I was able to tell when somebody was going through, or when somebody just wasn't feeling good in their body. I was so excited about this hospitality ministry.

Although serving the Lord in ministry was just fine with me; I still had the natural desires of a woman that wanted to be loved by a good man. And whenever the urge to date came upon me this time I used wisdom and I would submit to the leadership of my pastor and first lady and I would ask them first. Prayerfully, they would tell me yes, but most of the time they told me no, until I met the man who would become my husband. That's when all the nays went away.

Chapter 9

My Boaz

And Naomi had a kinsman of her husband's, a mighty man
of wealth, of the family of Elimelech; and his name was Boaz.
Then said Boaz unto his servant that was set over the reapers,
Whose damsel is this? So Boaz took Ruth,
and she was his wife…
Ruth 2:1,5,13

*I*n the book of Ruth, we find the account of a Moabite woman named Ruth. Ruth was the daughter in law of Naomi, a Jewish woman also living in Moab. Naomi had a husband and two sons. Both sons married wives from Moab. Ruth was married to one of the sons. Unfortunately, Naomi's husband died, and then Naomi's two sons died as well. Now both Ruth and Naomi are widows. Naomi felt that God's blessing was no longer on her. Feeling rejected and dejected Naomi decided to go back to Bethlehem-Judah to live out the rest of her sorrowful life. Naomi told her daughters-in-law, to stay there in Moab, but she would be returning to her country Judah. One of the daughters-in-law decided to stay in Moab, but as for Ruth this is what she had to say:

And Ruth said, Intreat me not to leave thee, or
to return from following after thee: for whither
thou goest, I will go; and where thou lodgest, I will
lodge: thy people shall be my people, and thy God
my God: Where thou diest, will I die, and there
will I be buried:

Ruth 1:16-17

Here Ruth's faithfulness and committed heart is demon-
strated. Ruth was a person who had gone through some
very difficult times and circumstances. But she was willing
to leave behind all her familiar surroundings, her comfort
zone, and way of life, so that she could stay by Naomi's side.
However, the most important aspect of Naomi's confession is
when she said, "thy people shall be my people, and thy God
my God." Ruth was willing to give up everything in order to
make the Lord, her God. Her heart was fixed, and it was
this mindset that caused her to walk right into God's plan
and purpose for her life. Ruth was set up to meet her soon
to be husband, Boaz. Boaz was a righteous man of God. He
was rich, powerful and was a man who commanded respect,
but he had no wife. However, according to God's divine plan
and in the fullness of time, God brought the two of them together to be part of an even bigger plan. And just like Ruth,
it was time for me to meet my Boaz, to fulfill God's bigger
plan for my life.

One day, my niece asked me if I wanted to take her on a
trip to Pentecostal Assemblies of the World (PAW) convention in Washington D.C. I told her no, I couldn't go because
I had recently moved into a new residence and I didn't have

any extra money to spend on an unplanned trip. However, my niece was insistent, practically begging, that we go to the PAW convention. Finally, her persistence paid off and I called one of the mothers of the church who was a travel agent. I explained to her that my niece was dying to go, but she didn't have any money. So I asked the travel agent, what is it that she could do with my limited budget? The travel agent said, "I'll tell you what. I'll pay your niece's way, but you pay your own way. We can save money by sharing a room. But you make sure your niece pays me back." So we were off to D.C. for the convention.

After getting nestled into our hotel accommodations, in Washington D.C., I received a copy of the convention events schedule. On that schedule was something that caught my attention. Each morning at seven o'clock, there was a worship service called the Prayer Clinic. Being the early riser that I am, I decided that I would like to start my day off by attending that service. There's something about meeting God early in the morning to start your day because you never know what God is going to do throughout the day. Little did I know at the time, God was setting me up a blessing—one that I could have never imagined would ever happen to me.

While attending the Prayer Clinic, I noticed this young man who couldn't seem to take his eyes off of me. He looked familiar because I had seen him around before at other PAW and church related events, but we had never officially met. The eye contact continued for the next few days, but the only conversation that we had was our "praise the

Lord," greetings. So the last night of the convention, there was a feeling of expectation turning in my spirit. I knew something was about to happen, but I didn't know what. So, in my heart I said to the Lord, "Lord, I don't want to just be pretty or sharp for somebody. I would love to be an angel for someone." And it was like the Lord was telling me, "Wear this. Put on that." It was truly amazing. God was interested in every little detail. Why? Because He was working out His master plan to bring me into my promised land.

When I came out my hotel room, it seemed like everyone was complementing me on how good I was looking. I could even hear people complementing me who weren't speaking directly to me as I walked by them.

Close to the convention hall, there was a cameraman on the side and he had pictures laid out. I went over there to try to just look at the pictures. He asked me if he could take my picture. I said, "I really don't want to take any pictures. I just want to come and look at your work." He took my picture anyway. I didn't like the picture, but I was there long enough for the man that had been admiring me throughout the convention, to walk up to the photographer's table. After seeing me, he immediately came over to me and asked how I was doing. I told him that I was doing fine. Then right out he asked me if I was married. I told him no. Then he asked me something that was a little strange, he asked me how was my baby. I responded, "Baby, that big old girl?"

He said, "Well, didn't you have a little baby?" Somewhat puzzled I responded, "No. Am I that fat or something?"

He started to laugh and responded saying, "No, you're not fat. I just thought you had a baby." "No, you got me mixed up with somebody else," I responded.

After that exchange, he walked away and went into this restaurant. I thought to myself, "Hmm that was a little strange." Later on, he told me that the Lord told him "You've been asking me about her. Now there she is. She let you know that she's available, she isn't married." He left out of the restaurant and came running back to the picture table. But I was already gone, heading out of the hotel.

As I was passing through the hotel lobby, I heard a man hollering out "Sister! Sister!" Of course, all the sisters turned around. But he was pointing at me. I waited for him. He said, "Sister I am so very much interested in you." While he was saying that he was interested in me, the Lord gave me a word for him, and I began to prophesy to him saying, "You did good but you didn't do great. In order for your ministry to go higher, you have to get rid of that malice in your heart for someone." When I said that, his eyes lit up and he responded saying "I know that God had to tell you that, because you don't know anything about me."

Right as I was prophesying to him, another brother in Christ that I knew came over to say hello to me. But this wasn't just any person, as God would have it, this was the very man that I had just prophesied about. As I spoke briefly to him, I could tell that my new admirer was not fond of him, because his countenance changed. So, as soon as this brother walked away, I looked right into my admirer's eyes and said, "he's the one you have the ought with isn't it?" Right when I asked him that he reached out to grab my hands. But, I pulled back. I didn't know him like that and I felt that he had no business trying to touch me.

While this was happening, one of my sisters in Christ who had seen what was going on also came over to me. Evidentially, when my admirer was yelling out to me it got her attention to. So, when she walked over to me, it was obvious that I was flustered because this man was putting me on the spot. She said, "Girl, go somewhere and pray," and that's what I did. So, I took off running and left him standing there.

I was confused. I had no way of knowing what kind of man he was. Then when my friend came up to me and said "go somewhere and pray," I didn't know if this was her way of saying that she knew something about this guy that I didn't know. However, that was my misinterpretation, because she wasn't at all telling me to leave him standing there. That's how my trip to the convention ended, on somewhat of a sour note. The next morning we left D.C. and came back to Chicago.

About a week or so had gone by since the D.C. convention. I had been in prayer about the whole matter. I told the Lord, "If a man is interested in me, he has to go all the way around the world to try to find me." I didn't want anybody else coming up to me and saying, "Hey baby, what's up? Can I get your number?" I didn't want any of that nonsense.

So one particular Tuesday, I came home from work exhausted. As I laid across the bed my telephone began to ring.

I had just moved into this place, so not too many people had my number. A man's voice was on the other end. I knew no man had my number. I said, "Hello." Then the man on the other end said, "I want to apologize to you on how I got your number," the voice on the other end said.

"Who is this," I asked.

Anthony Williams, he responded.

"I don't know anybody by that name," I replied. Then he said, "Pastor Anthony Williams." Now I knew who he was.

"Oh, you don't have to apologize to me. You had to get my number from a big shot because only big shots have my phone number," I lightheartedly responded.

I was talking about the two senior citizens that I called my spiritual mommas of the church. He caught my humorous drift and we both started laughing.

He then explained that both of our daughters used to call themselves sisters and were good friends, but we didn't know it. He asked his daughter if she would hurry up and get my number from my daughter. Apparently, his daughter wasn't moving fast enough for him. So, when one of the choir members heard about this, she said "Come on, boo, let me get your phone number because we are about to become cousins." I had always told my daughter not to ever give my phone number to grown people, but this time I'm glad that she disobeyed me.

As we began to converse, he asked me out on a date and he asked me what days did I have available. Mondays and Tuesdays were my usual days off or my slow days. I happened to be available on Tuesday. He said, "Let me look on my calendar and I can see when I can take you out."

I thought, "He got his nerve. I do not want no calendar man that has to schedule me in for a date." He said, "What about next Tuesday?" I'm saying to myself, "Now, I have to wait till Tuesday." But I told him, "Okay, no problem." So we hung up. He called me back less than thirty seconds later and said, "I can't wait that long." I was like, "Yes! Yes! Yes!" I was all excited. He asked me where I lived and I told him. He chose a restaurant near my home that I didn't even know was there because I had just moved in the area. It was a twenty-four-hour restaurant. So, I said okay and took him up on his invitation to go to dinner.

The next day I told my pastor about this brother wanting to take me out. My bishop said, "Well, there's nothing wrong with going out. You can go out, but be sure to check him out carefully." So that's exactly what I did.

Two weeks later, my pastor asked, "How did it go with the date?" "I'm still dating him," I anxiously responded.

He said, "Well you need to see me in my office." By that time, I had talked to Mr. Boaz and I told him, "bishop wants to see me in his office because I told him I was still dating you."

Mr. Boaz didn't tell me he called my bishop right after he hung up from me. He had told my bishop that there was a young lady in his congregation he was interested in and he would love to pursue her. My bishop had told him, "She's been through enough. She doesn't need anybody to come and try to hurt her heart."

Mr. Boaz told him, "You don't have to worry about that. I'm going to do everything I can to protect her. I'm going to do everything I can to help her. You don't have to ever worry about her ever having to come back to you in any kind of bad report about me."

I didn't know they were both negotiating and talking amongst each other without me even being in the midst of it. But I was also excited at the same time about the respect he had for my bishop and the respect that he had for me. I never had a man of this caliber.

So of course, I did not have to meet my bishop in his office because Mr. Boaz had already taken care of that for me. By the time he got off from work, he called me up and asked me if he could take me out to dinner. I lived on the third floor at that time. When I would step off the elevator, he would be standing on the passenger side of the car, opening the door. He was my chauffeur, just a handsome gentleman.

We went out every day. If we didn't do breakfast, we did lunch. If we didn't do lunch, we did dinner. If we didn't do dinner, we walked in the park, went to the movies, or just walked up and down the street holding hands. I would fix dinner for him and I and both of our daughters. We would come together as if we were one family. Both our girls were the only two kids left at home. Initially, there was some jealousy between them because they had to share their parents. But soon they adjusted and didn't get in each other's way.

The D.C. convention was in August. By October he asked me to marry him. I thought he was kidding. I started laughing. I was like, "Yeah, I sure will."

He said, "I'm not going to let nobody steal you away from me. I'm not going to let another brother have a chance to come back and try to get you. I am not leaving the door open for the enemy. I know what I want."

We went to this twenty-four-hour restaurant and talked for hours and hours. There was never a dry moment in the conversation. There was never quiet time in the conversation. I was enjoying him. He was enjoying me. I was looking at him. He was looking at me. We just enjoyed each other. After that first night there was no letting me get away.

We would talk on the phone for hours. When he would have to leave me, he would talk with me on the phone until I went to sleep on him. He said he never had a five hundred dollar phone bill before. He didn't care about any of that. He just had me grinning from ear-to-ear like I was a little high school girl all over again. It was so exciting.

One morning he called me about six-thirty or seven o'clock. He asked me what I was doing. I told him I was sleeping and you just woke me up. He said, "I'm on 95th Street and I need you to come out on the balcony. I'm on my way to work."

I said okay, hung up the phone and grabbed my robe. Soon he pulled up and stopped right in front of my apartment. He wanted to see what I looked like in the morning. So, when he pulled up he blocked traffic until I came out.

And when I did step out there on the balcony, of course the wind blew my robe. So he was able to get a little sneak peek. Evidently, he liked what he saw. I was still cute enough for him because he didn't ever stop coming around.

He was pursuing me. He taught me that a man is always supposed to pursue a woman, not the woman pursuing the man. I try to teach my daughters that naturally and spiritually.

I would always try to find something interesting to do. Even if it was nothing but going to get some ice cream together, that was fine with us. Since he worked downtown, that became our spot to hang out. He would take me to all the finest restaurants. I knew he was the one for me because there were times that I didn't want him to leave when it was time for us to part ways.

I felt safe with Mr. Boaz. I felt safe as if I was in the arms of the Lord. Even if I fell asleep, I would still be at peace. When I was riding with him, I was at peace. No matter what we did, if it was nothing but watching a movie, I felt comfortable. He'd leave and would say where he was going. I didn't have to worry about if he was coming back or not. I had no doubt in my mind that he was coming back. He was honest with me. Ninety percent of the time when he said he would do something, he definitely was going to do it or try his best to do it.

He didn't allow anybody to come in between us. We didn't allow anyone to try to dog one of us out. We spent so much quality time with each other and we knew each other so well that when other people did try to say something about me, he would say, "Let me go get her." Or vice versa, if somebody said something about him, I would say, "Let me go get him and ask him." They would change their mind. We knew then that they would be lying.

When God blesses you with something, He qualifies it. He equips it. You don't have to worry about turning your back on it. You don't have to second guess it. I told my first lady, "I'm really liking on him. What do you think?"

She said, "I tell you what, you don't have to go pray about it. You don't have to fast about it. He's the one." That's all I needed to hear because I made that mistake the first time of not going to my pastor or first lady first. I was not going to make that mistake ever again. But now, with the first lady's approval, it was like the Lord's confirmation that I too was to become a first lady.

My Boaz is a pastor, a good man, a blessed man, a called man, an anointed and appointed man in whom I love very much. Although it was a long time coming, it was well worth the wait. From the time we met to the time he proposed marriage, was only three short months. Truly, God did a short work in making me the pastor's wife.

Chapter 10

THE PASTOR'S WIFE

It's quite a transformation coming from a hustler's woman to being a pastor's wife. Being a pastor's wife is hard work. We have to know the Word of God. We are leaders yet servers. We have to guard access to our husbands, but at the same time, show great hospitality. We are great witnesses for the Lord. We go to the highways and the hedges to win souls for the Kingdom. We feed the homeless. We visit the sick. We mourn with the mourners, and we rejoice with those who rejoice. The love of Christ constrains us to do all these things. Yet Christ still gives us strength to tend to our own families and in some cases work full-time jobs or manage our own businesses. But no matter what we do, we do it as unto the Lord, because it is all a glorious assignment from heaven.

Unfortunately, there are many misconceptions about first ladies. Some people think that first ladies are there just to look good wearing our big hats and sharp clothes, but they do not see us working behind the scenes. They don't see all the hard work that goes into maintaining a church. Especially if the church is new, the first lady is a part of everything. First ladies are in the choir, on the usher board, and on the hospitality committee. We're on the clean-up crew, cleaning up around the church and making sure things are running properly. We are also fundraisers who come up with the needed finances when the lay members aren't paying their tithes and offerings.

I didn't know what to expect being a pastor's wife. I didn't know what to do. No one schooled me on the ins and outs of being a first lady. Whenever there are conventions, organizational meetings, and other gatherings of that nature, there is usually a time and place where pastors' wives come to sit and talk. At first, I didn't know that all this was part of being a first lady. I was new at this. No one told me the dos and don'ts. There wasn't anyone who said, "this is the way you're supposed to do it. This is what you shouldn't do. This is what you should do." No one ever rehearsed me in the so-called "first lady protocol." I had to find my way with the help of the Lord and the help of my husband.

The dynamics of each church is different. Though there are similarities, each first lady has a unique role at her own particular church. At our church, I had to learn quickly that I wasn't just a first lady. I was also a spiritual mother. The protocol issues were one thing, but the spiritual mother responsibility was another thing altogether. I had to realize that all these children coming into the sanctuary were my little babies, because God had set me as their spiritual mother. In the natural, I only wanted five children. However, I ended up with a multitude of children that keep me on my knees in prayer. I had to spend hours counseling some of these children and teens using a combination of mother's wit, tough love, and wisdom from God's Word. Though it is trying at times, I enjoy it because I know I am fulfilling my God-given purpose.

Another joy that I have as a pastor's wife is observing the spiritual growth of our young people. It was always so exciting to see young folks coming down aisles and giving their lives to the Lord. After being water baptized in Jesus' name, they would receive the gift of the Holy Ghost. After that, they would start coming to Bible study, joining the choir and helping out around the church. They would also participate in congregational events such as fasting and prayer services. They always kept me on my toes because they asked questions about everything. And if I didn't know the answer, I would tell them that I would find out and get back to them. They put quite a demand on me, but whenever I started feeling a little weary, I remembered how much help I needed when I got saved.

In our ministry, we really emphasize the importance of receiving the Holy Ghost. The Holy Spirit is essential in one's walk with the Lord. This is something that I knew for myself because I didn't have any power to live the Christian life on my own. I needed a helper. I needed a comforter. That's who the Holy Spirit is; He is our Comforter and our Helper. Without Him we could do nothing. In the past, that's why I kept doing the wrong things time and time again. I wanted to stop, but I didn't have the power to stop. However, once I received that Holy Ghost power, started reading the Bible, and began fasting and praying, my life began to change. I learned that I can do all things through Christ that strengthens me. Being sanctified and filled with the Holy Ghost, I knew that I could live a life that was pleasing to God. So that's what I teach to our young people, that you can do all things through Christ that strengthens you.

Being a first lady, is not something you can just walk into. God has to really equip you for being a pastor's wife. When God equips you, He knows you can handle it, but sometimes, we don't know it. It isn't always easy because people focus more on how they love their pastor. They look at the first lady like she's strange, and don't give her the respect that she deserves. Some of them try to marginalize her as if she wasn't important. But the power of prayer helps you get over becoming jealous and insecure. The power of prayer eventually makes them have to repent to the Lord and come back to you to apologize.

You have to do a lot of spiritual warfare in this position. You have to do a lot of fasting, so you can see what the pastor can't see from his perspective. I believe God gives the pastor's wife special discernment. He lets them observe all the sheep to see who belongs where. Everyone has a gift, but they must be functioning in the right place or else confusion starts.

I have learned that how many members a congregation has is not the most important thing. But no matter how many members you do have, you must be careful of who comes in amongst the flock. Especially, when people come from other churches to join, or even people who are newly saved. I always ask God, "Lord, did you send them or did Satan send them?" Satan can send you wolves in sheep's clothing. So to this day I always ask that question when people come into the ministry. I want to know if God sent them because if they do not belong to the Lord, they are not for us either.

Another thing that first ladies must confront is loneliness. Although there may be many people around you, being a pastor's wife can be a very lonely position. So many others walk right past you, to get the pastor's attention. And, if you are not careful, you may even feel a little intimidated. But when the pastor is on your side you have all the confidence that you need. Because, not only is he your leader and shepherd, but he is also your friend, and your lover. At the end of the day, he comes home to you because you are his wife, and you have the keys to his heart. It is a blessing when you have all of that in one package. Since the two of you are one, he can hear your heart and both of you can be of one mind. So, it doesn't matter what other people bring to you as long as you and your husband stand together as one. As the first lady, you get the best of both worlds, a dynamic pastor and a wonderful husband.

It is so important that first ladies fulfill their role as our husband's help-meet. It is our divine appointment to help our husbands meet their goals and responsibilities. As first ladies, we must be prayer partners with our husbands and lay hands on the pastor, praying for his strength in the Lord. We also carry out our husband's vision, to make sure he stays on task to help the vision come to pass, because we know that without a vision the people will perish. We do not want the man of God, to fall short of what God called him to do. We want him to keep trusting God, to help us to grow in grace. So that's when we go into our quiet place and lay before the Lord. We ask God to help him and to help us help him. I never want to be a source of embarrassment towards my husband, the Lord, or myself. So I fight daily in spiritual warfare to keep my body under subjection because that old hustler woman tries to rise up sometimes. And when those thoughts do come, I have learned how to pull down those strongholds through the power of the Holy Spirit. In the name of Jesus, I have the authority to rebuke the wiles of the devil.

People tend to think that those in church leadership are somehow exempt from the troubles of this life. We're not. We have good days and bad days just like the rest of the people. We just try not to show ours because we want to keep the other people encouraged. We want to keep the congregation lifted up. We want to see our folks growing in the Lord and prospering, and praying always that God keeps them from harm and danger. But the reality is, people get into all sorts of trouble. And just like a mother agonizes over her natural children, so does the first lady when her spiritual children fall from grace.

You get disappointed when they backslide. You get disappointed when they act as if they never knew the Lord. You invest a lot of time and effort in them, so when they turn their back on the church (God is really the one they're turning their back on) it hurts you too. But you still continue to pray that the grace of God does not leave them. And you pray that God has mercy on them so that they will come back into the ministry.

When I see some of them on the street, I don't beat them down. I just say, "Momma still loves you. Are you in anybody's church?" They might say yes, or maybe sometimes they say no, and I say, "You are always welcome to come on back home. Daddy and I are going to be there with opened arms and glad to see you. Don't let the enemy lie to you; we aren't going to beat you up. It's the devil who really wants to harm you because you are in the world and outside of the ark of safety. The world hates you just like it hated Jesus. We know because, at one time, we have been out there too. It's not necessary to go through what we went through. But our job is to encourage you to come back home."

Sometimes they come back. Sometimes they stay out there. But I never stop believing God that they will come back home or find another good ministry to go to. Though we watch out for their souls, none of them really belongs to us. Often, God has different people to have an impact on a child of God's life. As the apostle Paul teaches, "I have planted, Apollos watered; but God gave the increase" (1 Co. 3:6).

As pastors' wives, even at our weakest moment, we have to keep our head lifted up to the hills because we know that our help always comes from the Lord. Even when we are tired and want to throw in the towel, we have to remember who holds our future. We have to remember who promised us that He will never leave or forsake us. We have to remember that we can carry all our burdens to the Lord in prayer because God cares for us.

Pastor's wives must be kept up before the Throne of Grace because of their unique assignment. We are the pastor's supporters when no one else will. We are the under girders when all others give up. When God called the pastor, He also called the pastor's wife, because the average woman could never deal with all the pressures of being a first lady unless she was called to it. And every challenge that we face is not always the devil, as we like to say. Some of it is the work of the flesh like jealousy from other women in the church, who would love to knock you off your square and take your man. These challenges and confrontations are all a part of dealing with people. It's all a part of the calling. But once the first lady fully embraces her calling despite all the difficulties, the ministry will grow, the pastor will be strengthened; the whole church will prosper. As the saying goes, "Everybody is happy when momma is happy."

One of my secrets for success is I try to find the good in everyone. Even when they're in a bad situation that seems like they can't break free, I try to encourage them and let them know that nothing is impossible. God is the Master at taking many broken pieces and creating masterpieces. I try to encourage them by letting them know that God has need of them, if they would just open up their hearts and allow God to do His work in them. I know when God has us on the potter's wheel, things can get uncomfortable as He shapes us. But as you let Him work, how much more peace you would have because God does everything well.

Yes, I love being God's servant. I am truly living a blessed life. Today, I sing unto the Lord a new song. And even though I love my husband, I can't put him before God. God has brought me through too much. I was living in darkness for too long, even though I may have looked like I was living the high life, I was a miserable wretch. But today I can say that God pulled me out of darkness and into the marvelous light. I was ashamed of the things that I did, the people that I associated with, and the places I use to go. But now, I'm not ashamed to tell my story, because the Bible says that we overcome the devil by the blood of the Lamb and the word of our testimony (Rev. 12:11).

In Hebrews 11:31, and James 2:25, the Bible refers to Rahab, as "Rahab the Harlot." Clearly, after the fall of Jericho, Rahab was no longer a prostitute. But her former occupation played a role in God's plan for her life. Rahab displayed great faith when she hid Israel's spies. Because of her faith, God saved Rahab and her family and gave her a new identity. Rahab married Salmon, and they had a son, his name was Boaz. Boaz married Ruth, and they had a son named Obed. Obed had a son and his name was Jessie. Jessie had seven sons; the youngest was David. Fourteen generations from David came Jesus, who was Son of God and also the son of David. Jesus, the Lord of glory, had a gentile prostitute in his earthly bloodline through his mother Mary. Though I was not a prostitute like Rahab, I was still an unchaste woman whom

God chose to save and place in His royal family too. What a mighty God we serve! Cain't nobody do you like Jesus!

A LABOR OF LOVE

When my husband and I started out together as pastor and wife, we had a small congregation of about twelve members. However, the Lord has blessed us to have so many children, some of them have moved on from state to state and city to city, but they started right here with us. When they come back home, they visit us. I have prayed for people over the telephone in other states to receive the power of the Holy Ghost. People have received the Holy Ghost right there in my beauty salon. It's a ministry when people come into the salon. I have prayed in the grocery store for people to be healed. Wherever God saw a need, and I was there, I was not afraid to launch out into the deep, especially when I know that they need the power. The first thing I would ask them is do you have that power? When they ask, what power are you talking about? I would answer the power of the Holy Ghost. That's the power that they need to come out of that destructive lifestyle that is leading them to hell. It is the love of God that causes me to compel people everywhere to come to the Lord.

The community where our church edifice is located is an under-served high crime area. However, it is a lighthouse in this otherwise dark environment. We have transformed our old church building from a lifeless brick building with no purpose or vision, to a safe haven for hope and restoration.

And from that very location, God has used Labor of Love Apostolic Church to change the lives of hundreds of people for the better. At one time the vineyard had dried up but now the Lord sent laborers into this vineyard to revitalize and restore this community on the east-side of Chicago.

Yes, we still face challenges daily, and there are times when it seems like our ministry is not making a difference in that community. And that's exactly what the enemy wants us to think just to discourage us. However, we know there has been a change because so many souls have given their lives to the Lord. We have seen women come out of prostitution. We have seen people get delivered from drugs. We have seen inmates released from prison. We have seen people who used to carry guns and knives, carrying their Bibles and placing their trust in the Lord. It's truly exciting to see people being transformed right before our eyes, and to know that the Lord has used you to be a part of their growth and change.

All along, the Lord knew that this is where I would be. It's the only reason that I have made it from such a destructive life. So I end this book with the full assurance that God has foreordained and predestinated my life. All the years of my wandering I never strayed too far away for God's loving arms to save me. Through the situations and circumstances that I have experienced, God was never taken by surprise, but He patiently stood at the door of my heart and knocked, until I opened up and let him in. Once I did that, everything changed, and my true identity and purpose was revealed. I am truly a new creation in Christ Jesus. Like the popular Gospel song says, "I never would have made it," without the Lord on my side.

And finally, my sisters and brothers, I would like to leave you with this: there is no God like the living God. Truly, our God is an awesome God but, He is no respecter of persons. What He did for me, He will do it for you too, because His goodness and mercy endures forever. Only God could have taken me from being a hustler's woman, and made me to be a pastor's wife.

The End

THE PLAN OF SALVATION

On the day of Pentecost, the Jews asked Peter this most important question, "what must we do to be saved?" Peter answered and said, "Repent everyone one of you, and be baptized in the name of Jesus Christ, for the remission of sins, and you shall receive the gift of the Holy Ghost" (Acts 2:38). There is nothing you can do to earn salvation. It is a gift that God gives to anyone who calls on the name of Jesus. You can be saved right now, if you pray this prayer with a truly repentant heart, God will save you.

> Father God, in the name of Jesus, I believe that Jesus Christ is the Son of God. He died for my sins on Calvary's cross. I believe that He rose again from the dead on the third day. And I believe that if I confess with my mouth that Jesus is Lord, and believe in my heart that God has raised Him from the dead, that I shall be saved. Jesus, I believe it, and I receive you as my Lord and my savior. Thank, you for saving me, and writing my name in the Lamb's Book of Life. In Jesus' mighty name, Amen.

Now that you have prayed this prayer, find a Bible believing church and be baptized in Jesus' name, so you too will be filled with the precious gift of the Holy Ghost. May God bless and keep you always. If you are in the Chicago area and need a church home you are welcome to join us at:

The Labor of Love Apostolic Church
District Elder Anthony Williams, Sr., Pastor
2800 E. 79th Street
Chicago, IL 60649
(773) 734-7207

LIFE TO LEGACY, LLC

Let us bring your story to life! With Life to Legacy, we offer the following publishing services: manuscript development, editing, transcription services, ghostwriting, cover design, copyright services, ISBN assignment, worldwide distribution, and eBooks.

Throughout the entire production process, you maintain control over your project. We are here to serve you. Even if you have no manuscript at all, we can ghostwrite your story for you from audio recordings or legible handwritten documents.

We also specialize in family history books, so you can leave a written legacy for your children, grandchildren, and others. You put your story in our hands, and we'll bring it to literary life! We have several publishing packages to meet all your publishing needs.

Call us at: 877-267-7477, or you can also send e-mail to: Life2Legacybooks@att.net. Please visit our Web site: www.Life2Legacy.com

CPSIA information can be obtained at www.ICGtesting.com
Printed in the USA
LVOW13s1159140714

394205LV00001B/2/P